Published by **Enete Enterprises**

1321 Upland Dr. Houston, TX 77043 (USA)

1st Edition of

Life Another Way: Living Your Dreams

I0167796

Enete, Shannon, 2017

Life Another Way / Shannon Enete

ISBN: 1-938216-19-9
ISBN: 978-1-938216-19-0

Printed in the United States of America
www.EneteEnterprises.com

OTHER BOOKS BY THIS AUTHOR

☑ Earn an Income Abroad
☑ Becoming an Expat Ecuador
☑ Becoming an Expat Costa Rica
☑ Becoming an Expat Thailand
☑ Becoming an Expat Mexico
☑ Becoming an Expat 101
☑ Becoming a Nomad
☑ Teeth Not Tears: Smiles Through the Rubble

DEDICATION

This book was written for all of you who don't want to live a M-F office job and who have a restless sense of adventure lurking beneath the surface. I also want to thank my love, Gina Castagnozzi, for her unwavering support.

TABLE OF CONTENTS

INTRODUCTION

You aren't stuck. Every decision is a choice, even the decision to "not make a decision" and stay put. In order for you to understand what this program is all about, I'm going to share with you Life Another Way's Mission, Vision, and Values.

Mission

To motivate and guide "sleep-living" people to live with a purpose-filled passion-driven life. We provide the tools necessary to design your dream life in a one month, 1 year, or a 5 year plan and take ACTION to achieve it. We achieve our goal when you achieve yours.

Vision

To be the leading source (a means to an end) for those who are looking to live *Life Another Way.* Support each other through an active and kind forum. (Trolls won't be tolerated.) We will host an interactive life discussion or workshop biweekly. We will remain liquid, constantly improving the program and the process plus you can look forward to our annual retreats.

Values

We value ACTIONS over words. A supportive environment is fed by honesty, encouragement, creativity, and individual growth. We have no room for haters.

Simply put, we are going to teach you how to create a plan of action to move yourself into your dream life. With technology today, there is no reason why you can't live in your favorite spot in the world, or why you can't search for that special place while earning an income. Don't worry, we'll teach you about the technology and how to best utilize it for your goals.

There is no one correct way to live, only the best way for you. Our program is designed to help you discover what makes you tic, and what lifestyle brings out the best you. Then we have a ACTIONABLE plan that will get you there! We will help you break down your goals into small steps that get the job done.

I can't tell you how often I hear, "Must be nice to travel all the time… I wish I could do that." or a variety of excuses stopping them, but they are just that— excuses. Life Another Way will teach you how to change your mentality, thought habits, redesign your attitude, and stifle your fear in order to have the confidence to get where you'd like to go. We even help you figure out where exactly that is!

WHAT TO EXPECT- *an overview*

1. Changing Your Course

- Overview, life recipe, endless possibilities, examples of counter normal lifestyles, active decision making (designing your life), and the integration of balance
- Retrain your brain (explode the box), attitude, habits designed for success, and mistakes and how they are managed
- Addressing fear, flexibility, and self acceptance

2. Taking Action

- Setting your priorities: make choices every single day that reflect those priorities; financially, ethically, and socially.
- Setting goals for today, tomorrow, next month, next year. What can I do today to change my life path? What can I do tomorrow to start a new habit? What is my long term goal right now? Keep in mind flexibility and reassessing goals. Simplify wherever possible
- Surrounding yourself with positivity: the myth about selfishness
- Time Management: everyone has the same number of hours in a day, learn to say NO
- No more excuses
- Visualization and clarity

3. Taking care of yourself physically and mentally

- Workouts / Active Lives
- Eating right
- Meditation
- Yoga
- Starting your day right- habits built for success

4. Jobs, entrepreneurship, legalities, and finances

- Logistics for moving abroad: travel vs expat, legalities, finances, etc
- Logistics for working on the road: technology, focusing while touring
- Remote career vs. starting a business
- Social media 101, working remotely, time management and goal management – in a work/money context
- Logistics for couples travel vs solo travel: safety, compromise, finances, etc
- Budgeting & Banking

5. Reassess and repeat

- Managing your goals: constantly check back in with yourself
- Flexibility is the key to happiness. Find your balance now, and then be willing to change it. Never say never.

* Package add ons: Families/ furry, Nomad, Expat, Snow Birding, RVing

HOW TO USE THIS CURRICULUM

Congratulations for taking the first step in your Life Another Way! Let me breakdown how this program works. The book is only actionable if you take action. It will serve you best if you complete all of the worksheets and actionable steps. This package is designed for each type of learner. If you're a visual learner like myself, you can focus on the video tutorials as your primary learning method then use either the written curriculum or the audible mp3s to really send the message home. If you are reading the paperback version you can find all multimedia at www.lifeanotherway.com. We've all heard that it takes hearing any singular message three times before it's ingrained in our memory, so feel free to use each learning method or one three times!

In addition to the curriculum and worksheets, you have access to a forum filled with peers in the program, a built-in support system and, of course, me. If you enroll in the online interactive course at http://academy.lifeanotherway.com then our coaches will answer your questions and provide guidance. Please record your weekly progress as a running log in the online forum. This will help you record your growth, goals, and accomplishments, and at the same time you can receive "atta boys" from your peers. Finally, take advantage of our live workshops and Q&A sessions. Learn from special guests with various specialties that are sure to impact your growth. It's going to be a good time, but if you can't attend the live session, not to worry, you will have access to the recorded versions.

Life Another Way is not just a program. It's a community, a lifestyle, and the constant for you in your journey. After all, it's the

journey that is most important. Check in every week or so at
www.LifeAnotherWay.com to see what new resources we've
added for you.

NO TROLLS
It's important to note that we have a zero tolerance for "trolls" (those who post negative, argumentative, or aggressive comments). You will be banned from the forum if your actions conflict with our **L.A.W of the land**.

THE L.A.W. OF THE LAND

1. Give your life and this academy 100%
2. Be impeccable with your word
3. Never make assumptions
4. Don't take things personally
5. Have unwavering faith in yourself and your goals
6. Be supportive and interactive with the Life Another Way community
   * One negative or attacking remark in the community and you will be banned
7. Follow your passions
8. Be creative
9. Love and allow love into your life
10. Be kind to yourself
11. Create your new life by following passion and love rather than running away from a feeling of lacking
12. Always be grateful
13. Live the best life you can
14. There is always a way
15. We never leave our wingman/woman- you're not in this alone! You have an entire community to connect with and pair up into wingmen/women

RETRAIN YOUR BRAIN

THE PURSUIT OF PASSION

Your biggest hurdle is most likely you. That's why I've dedicated an entire section to your philosophy and attitude. Feeling stuck is 100% mental. We're rarely truly stuck, nor can we stay exactly where we are in mind and spirit. Life is fluid. So we need to train ourselves to be flexible and to work change in our favor.

Overall, I've been a very confident and determined individual. After a career-ending back injury, some of my confidence wavered. I functioned at the top of my peer group as a paramedic and without the consistent ego strokes, my confidence slowly waned. This caused a shift in my inner dialog and subconscious. Fear slid its ugly head into my life in a more powerful way than ever before. I found myself questioning every move I made: will it be profitable, will I fail? The *fear of failure* steered my decisions instead of *passion and the pursuit of doing good*. After battling this shift, learning more about myself, and the journey of life, I stumbled upon some amazing tools that helped me rediscover my voice and the courage to execute what I believed in.

Before I share this with you, I highly suggest that you find a buddy or wingman/woman that can help you in your pursuit for awesome. Feel free to connect with others in the program in our forum, or see if your spouse or close friend is interested in signing up for the program so you can be wingmen.

The following "agreements" are game changers. Make sure you give each one the time and open-mindedness it deserves.

THE FOUR AGREEMENTS

The Four Agreements is not only a book I recommend reading, but a philosophy of life. To put it simply, much of our pain is unknowingly caused by us. The book states what you believe about yourself is an "agreement" you have chosen to accept. For example, if my dad told me I was awesome at math a few times, I probably would have accepted that agreement believing that yes, I was indeed a math rockstar! I would look for any opportunity to reaffirm this belief to myself and to him. This extra effort would in-fact increase my math ability since I would study harder and look for more opportunities to excel. However, this rule swings the other way frequently. If my sister said I had a horrible singing voice, I could choose to accept this agreement and reaffirm it through my inner dialog.

Our actions and agreements with ourselves can either build us up or tear us down. The philosophy in *The Four Agreements* dives pretty deep claiming that my reality is not the same as your reality so why should I worry about your perception of me? It's kinda heavy, and may not be for everyone. The critical takeaways, however, are the four agreements themselves and the practice of replacing unhealthy false agreements with new uplifting ones.

"True justice is paying only once for each mistake.
True injustice is paying more than once for each mistake."
~ The Four Agreements

1. ALWAYS DO YOUR BEST

No matter what you're doing right now, do it to the best of your ability. This doesn't mean perfection, actually not even close. It means doing your best with the amount of energy, resolve, and skills you have right now. Your best will fluctuate every hour, day, year, and task.

By doing your best in every instance, you can discredit and avoid self-judgement, self-abuse, and regret. After all, how can you expect to do more than your best? Your productivity, happiness, energy, and resolve are in constant flux. Do your best with what you have at any given moment and decide that your best is always enough.

My work cycle is just that, cyclic. There are days I'm exceptionally productive, I can't type fast enough to keep up with the creation in my mind. I might feel so inspired I work a few 12 hour days in a row, then I dry up and feel uninspired for a couple of days. I understand my workflow and allow myself to ride the waves because it's what makes me most happy. If I try to force myself into a 9-5 each day, it serves no one. I do the best with my creative juices and don't force it. If your work doesn't allow this type of flexibility and you feel like you would thrive *with* this type of flexibility, it may be time to search elsewhere for work (see the: **Work Remotely** & **Start a Business From Anywhere** modules). If you want to dive deeper read the book I recently released, Earn an Income Abroad.

The same goes for our social lives. You've probably already figured out the rough amount of social engagement you need to satiate the connection you need as a human being. Do you allow yourself this amount, or do you constantly overload your social fix because you can't say no? Doing your best means doing the best for you, not for everyone else. If you thrive with one social get together a week, don't say yes to three. In this instance doing your best can mean saying no to situations that will throw you off your A game. Learn more about **Saying No** in the corresponding section later in this academy.

2. BE IMPECCABLE WITH YOUR WORD

Your words matter. The old saying *"Sticks and stones may break my bones, but words will never hurt me..."* well, *your* words will hurt you if they aren't impeccable. Speak with a high moral compass, integrity, and honesty. Say only what you mean and don't use language as a means of manipulation. Be "that guy" or "that girl" people say doesn't have a negative word to utter about anyone. Avoid gossip like the plague. This will be very difficult for some, but it's possible and the work is worth it. Gossiping can rot your soul and produces nothing but negativity, judgment, and shallowness. Instead, use your words to direct love and your inner convictions.

When you are confronted with gossiping friends, you have a variety of methods to manage the situation:

✦**Avoidance** (the run away method)— Yup, this one is the "I hear my mom calling" tactic.
✦**Redirect**— Squirrel! It's easy to redirect the conversation with a well timed compliment, story, or recommendation of a funny movie you just watched.
✦**Play devil's advocate**— Argue for the person that is being talked about. Offer other points of view on the same circumstance, and remind you, friends they don't know the whole story or all of the facts about the person they are smashing.
✦**Confrontation**— *"I like* insert name *so I'm not going to talk about her/him. Let's talk about something else."* You can also remind the gossiper of the nice things the person has done for them or said about them.

3. DON'T MAKE ASSUMPTIONS

This is a huge problem with today's communication methods. Since it's become isolated to written shorthand via text message, Facebook, and 140 character tweets, there is endless room for assumptions and speculation. Take the time to clarify, ask questions, and followup. Be a straight shooter. Most people appreciate honesty, and the boldness it takes to ask direct questions. If you find someone who doesn't appreciate it, well that's more their problem than yours.

Try to communicate as much as possible in person or over the phone. Just because others communicate digitally does not mean you're confined to that method. With clear communication, you can avoid misunderstandings and countless gray hairs from the drama that would have ensued.

4. DON'T TAKE ANYTHING PERSONALLY

We are a self-absorbed people, nothing others do is solely because of you. No two realities (experiences in life) are the same. Therefore, what others say and do is reflective of their reality, not yours. Even if you don't buy into this philosophy, what people say and do is based on their experiences and perceptions, how their day has gone, what agreements they have made with themselves, how they were raised, and you simply crossed paths with them. If they lash out, it likely has nothing to do with you, but what you represent to them. Repeat the last sentence out loud. When you can take this message to heart and remind yourself of it daily, you will save yourself much needless suffering.

"We have learned to live our lives trying to satisfy other people's demands. We have learned to live by other people's points of view because of the fear of not being accepted and of not being good enough for someone else."
~ The Four Agreements

TAKING ACTION

Write your new affirmations on stickies and put them on your mirror, computer, and/or refrigerator. Repeat one new affirmations every morning, lunchtime, and bedtime until you truly agree, then move on to a new affirmation.

ACTIONABLE TIPS

Clean House-
"You are the average of the five people you spend the most time with" ~ Unknown

One of the best tips I can give you is to surround yourself with loving supportive friends and family. Tell them your goals, and ask for help. In the beginning of your journey, identifying your counterproductive habits is key. Your loved ones can help remind you of your goals if you're gossiping, making assumptions, taking things personally, etc. Soon enough you'll begin to filter not only your actions and speech but you thoughts. When you find that your thoughts are not in "agreement" with your new agreements, don't judge or persecute yourself. Simply dismiss the thought and replace it with a positive agreement. For example, if my inner dialog says, "You're going to fail" simply interrupt yourself and say, *"Actually, I have the drive, skills, ambition, and personality to make this a huge success, and that is what I will do."* Even if you don't 100% believe those words, through repetition and a positive attitude, you will soon.

If you don't clean house of the negative people who bring you down, it will be infinitely more difficult to replace your negative thoughts with positive ones, especially if you're surrounded with a straight stream of negativity.

Choosing positive people to spend time with also helps in your effort to be impeccable with your word. I'm sure you've noticed that you pick up sayings, slang and other mannerisms from those you spend the most time with. If those people exhibit qualities that you are aspiring toward, you're on the right path. Because, after all, *"You are the average of the five people you spend the most time with"* so pick your five wisely.

TAKING ACTION
Change your passwords to affirmations. For instance, after I ended a 5.5 year relationship, I changed my passwords to: itwillgetbetter. Come up with a few affirmations and cycle through one each week or each month. Just make sure you write down the current password in your journal or other safe spot so you won't lose it.

Worksheet 1.1

The Four Agreements

Think about your skill set. What agreements have you made with yourself about your natural given gifts?

_____
_____
_____
_____
_____
_____
_____
_____
_____
_____
_____
_____
_____
_____
_____
_____
_____
_____
_____
_____
_____

What old agreements have you made about what is possible for you and your life?

_____
_____
_____
_____
_____
_____
_____
_____
_____
_____
_____
_____
_____
_____
_____
_____
_____

What new agreements do you commit to make today? Where do you want your life to go? What skills would you like to develop?

_____
_____
_____
_____
_____
_____
_____
_____
_____
_____
_____

List the people in your life who are supportive of your goals and who have a positive attitude. People who align well with the person you are becoming.

_____
_____
_____
_____
_____
_____
_____
_____
_____

List the people who are negative and bring you down, or do not align with the best you.

_____
_____
_____
_____
_____
_____
_____
_____
_____

Look at the two sets of people and consider the amount of time you spend with each, see if you need to make any adjustments in order to live your Life Another Way. Are they the right five?

Focus on solutions, not problems.

There are instances where you're forced to pair-up with negative people. In those situations be extra mindful where and how you focus your attention because it will determine your emotional state. Focusing on the problems you or your coworker are facing will prolong negative emotions and stress. If you focus on actions that can improve your circumstances, you create a sense of power that yields feel good fuzzies and a reduction in stress.

Therefore, fixating on how miserable your co-worker (or other negative person you are forced to endure) only intensifies your suffering by giving them power over you. Instead focus on how you're going to go about handling their behavior in a positive way, or better yet focus on your behavior and your present moment. This places you in the driver's seat, and returns the power of your happiness to it's rightful owner, you.

*Optional for Facebook Users:

Make sure you remove and/or unfollow negative people on your Facebook. Once this is complete, post one new agreement you've made with yourself.

VISUALIZATION

Picture it now… There is something very powerful about visualizing the best version of you. It's encouraging, motivating, and some believe cosmically powerful. Regardless of your beliefs, utilizing our guided meditations and visualizations at the beginning and end of your day will lead you to your dream life. I like to tell people, *"What you see is what you get"* when speaking about my personality, however that statement is also true about what you envision for yourself. You don't have to believe in this philosophy, just try it and see if it makes you feel energized, at peace, or better in any way. If so, then commit to starting and/or ending your day with one of our included visualizations.

* **ACTION:** Listen to the guided meditation titled- *Your Guardian Angel.* Afterwards complete worksheet 1.2.

WORKSHEET 1.2

Your Guardian Angel Meditation

After listening to *Your Guardian Angel,* write down what your guardian angel looked like, acted like, said, and anything else remarkable to you.

_____
_____
_____
_____
_____
_____
_____
_____
_____
_____
_____
_____
_____
_____
_____
_____
_____
_____
_____
_____
_____
_____
_____
_____
_____
_____

WWMGAD?

Everything you do today, ask yourself, what would my guardian angel do? With each choice, decide if it will lead to becoming the best you. Also, test the decision against the agreement, "Always do my best."

ATTITUDE

"Keep your thoughts positive because your thoughts become YOUR WORDS. Keep your words positive because your words become YOUR BEHAVIOR. Keep your behavior positive because your behavior becomes YOUR HABITS. Keep your habits positive because your habits become YOUR VALUES. Keep your values positive because your values become YOUR DESTINY."
~ Mahatma Gandhi

A poor attitude yields poor outcomes, a rich attitude leads to a rich life. Who is your negative attitude serving? You? Certainly not! Can you think of one good thing it's gotten you? Ask your loved ones how it impacts them when you are negative. If they're honest, you'll likely hear that when you're negative, you can be difficult to be around. It's like breathing in the smog-filled air, polluting their minds.

"Every thought we think is creating our future." ~ Louise Hay
"The mind is everything. What you think you become." ~ Buddha

A rich life is one where you thrive and are happy. While this might include monetary riches, it doesn't have to if that's not part of your pursuit for happiness. ***If you take the time you normally use to magnify what you're lacking and the negative in your life and decide to use that time to focus on gratitude and what you're working toward, you will see a true transformation***. Good begets good. Your positive attitude will not only bring you more happiness and freedom in your mind but will open up opportunities and connections you would never establish as a negative Nancy.

26

"Whether you think you can, or think you can't, you're right."
~ Henry Ford

It's hard to believe, but attitude is a choice. How you choose to view and respond to circumstances is a choice. Sometimes it doesn't feel like one, but with practice you will hone the skill of slowing down your reactions enough to decide which reaction is best.

Hal Elrod, who we mention in **Creating Habits Destined For Success**, taught me the three key components to a successful attitude: unwavering faith, extraordinary effort, and the following affirmation for each goal you set out to achieve: *"I will do (insert goal), I have to do (insert goal), there is no other way."*

Hal's Trifecta

Unwavering Faith

Just as you believe your new agreements, you need to have unwavering faith that you will accomplish your goals even if at first you don't believe the affirmation (below). Keep repeating it and soon you will believe it. Believing in yourself is paramount. No matter how much a spouse or loved one may believe in you, if you don't have faith in yourself, expect a self-fulfilling prophesy.

Extraordinary Effort

Whether you hail from the hard-working baby boomers or the laissez faire millennials, you have to put in sweat equity to accomplish YOUR goals and YOUR best life. Think about it… What else would you want to put 100% effort into? This is not a math course you think you'll never need again, this is a course on how to live your best life according to YOU! So don't half ass it!

Repeating the Affirmation: *"I will do (insert goal), I have to do (insert goal), there is no other way."*

If this affirmation doesn't work for you, create another one. I have a hard time trying to tell myself that I *have* to do something and that there is *no other way*. Especially when I know there are numerous routes to any given result. It goes against my personality. I'm a freedom fighter and I answer to no one. So instead, I use, *"I will (insert goal), I am (insert goal), and it's amazing."* I also like, *"I have the drive, skills, ambition, and personality to make this a huge success, and that is what I will do."* Whichever affirmation you choose, say it with fervor. Picture a sports team getting revved up for a big game. Their coach delivers a motivating speech, and they start bouncing in a huddle, ready to explode with purposeful energy that is sure to accomplish their goal of crushing their opponents. Now apply that emotional buildup to your goal. Get amped when you repeat your affirmation, jump around, roar, pound your chest, do a happy dance, or slide on the wood floor in your socks and underwear risky business style. Do whatever it takes to get you psyched!

It will blow your mind to see what you can accomplish when you decide you're capable and dedicate the effort to get there.

TAKE RESPONSIBILITY FOR YOURSELF

You are the only one who is responsible for you and the only one who will take care of you. Do not hand over your happiness, life choices, or career to someone else. When I was sixteen, I remember getting super sick while at work. I kept thinking the manager would see how miserable I was and send me home. After I threw up multiple times and he had no concern to take action, I learned it was no one else's responsibility to take care of me. I told him I was sick and needed to go home, and thus got myself the rest I needed to heal. By placing your wellbeing and health into someone else's hands, you assign yourself a victim's role. No matter what he/she/they choose to do for your wellbeing, you can react with sadness and dismay. Avoid this at all cost! Making someone else responsible for you equals drama, pain, suffering, and a trapped feeling. Why give away your power and outsource your happiness?

"If you don't design your own life plan, chances are you'll fall into someone else's plan. Guess what they have planned for you? Not much."
~ Jim Rohn

For those of you with this tendency, create a list of ways this has served you and a list of ways it has hurt you. This list should serve as motivation enough to change your behavior, but just in case it isn't, answer me this question: "If you want to redesign your life to become the best you, how can you do that without access to your power and happiness?"

TAKING RESPONSIBILITY FOR YOUR LIFE

"My 7 siblings and I, grew up in a home of "victims". What I mean by that is, yes we were abused (sexually, physically, & emotionally), yes my parents got divorced and my father had hardly any communication with us, and, yes, it was difficult. BUT we allowed those things to define us and stop us from growing healthy, getting the education we needed and becoming successful adults. We would say things like "I'm hurt so I don't want to do this or that", I'm angry, so I shouldn't have to do this", "It's their fault for the bad decisions I'm currently making." etc. Not in those words necessarily, but in our actions. We were mad at the world, and we wanted everyone to know it, so we wreaked havoc everywhere we went. We did drugs, abused alcohol, were promiscuous, were in gangs, I was a run away....there is a LONG laundry list! WHAT IF we had said, "Yes this happened, but we can still get an education.", or "Yes, it happened, but that doesn't mean I can't graduate high school or go to college.", or "Yes, I'm angry, but I don't have to allow my anger to control me.", or "Yes, it hurt, but I can forgive, let it go, and be better off by doing so."? What if we shifted our thinking and didn't allow our victimization to dictate our future or to lead us to victimize ourselves through adolescence and early adulthood and or become the perpetrators ourselves carrying on a long family tradition?

Taking responsibility... One of the most pivotal moments/decisions in my life.

When I was 18 I fell in love with Ryan, my now husband of 13 years. He was so different than I was. His outlook was of optimism instead of pessimism. He was educated. His parents were still married and in love. His parents treated him very well, always believed in him, and it was obvious how different we were, that's honestly one of the things I liked most about him (Side note: I had only dated losers up to this point. People who treated me like dirt, yet I had allowed it). About a year in of Ryan and I dating, we moved from Arizona, where my brother, grandparent, aunts, uncles and cousins were, to Oklahoma so he could finish his college education at OSU. For the first time in my life I was away from my family. I did not realize how codependent I was to my family. I didn't realize how dramatic my family was until I started seeing the other side of the spectrum. My husband found good, healthy friendships. People who didn't complain about everything. People who were going to college, had life plans and goals, and were happy. Not that I wasn't "happy", I loved Ryan, and I was "happy", but not "healthy happy".

There was a strong learning curve. After being away from my family and around healthy people stuff really started to bug me. I didn't know how to fit in. I needed to learn a healthy way to deal with my emotions, I needed a healthy perspective on relationships. I started counseling and worked harder than ever to fit in with his healthy friends. It took me 2 ½ years to combat the 19 years of victimization/perpetration"

~ Feliz, Oklahoma

Stealth Giveaway

You can give away your power and happiness without even knowing it. Those who live for the **approval of others** have done just that. Have your decisions or course in life been chosen in part to appease or please someone else? If so, you're not alone. This is one of the most common problems when recreating your Life Another Way

Love and *approval* are separate entities. For example, if you have an overbearing or "extra-loving" parent who interferes in your life, you need to train them how to best love you. After all, his/her goals are usually innocent, but when you allow them the authority to redirect or dictate your path, you are cultivating a habit harmful to both you and your relationship. It's up to you to set boundaries. You know best about your happiness. While you don't welcome their opinions about how you should live your life, you do appreciate support for YOUR choices.

Whenever I think of this lesson, I can't help but think about the popular American sitcom, *Everyone Loves Raymond*. Zero boundaries are enforced and a plethora of resentment builds up between each family member. While it's not real, I'm willing to bet you or someone you know have similarly intrusive family members. It's never too late to set boundaries. Sit down with your loved one and explain to them that you're on a mission to become the best you possible and you need their help. *"I appreciate your care, concern, and all of your guidance over the years. It's part due to your support that I'm ready to take the next step and lead my life based on my convictions right or wrong. Here is how you can help me achieve my goals:…"* List your new boundaries / needs from them.

For example, if you have relatives or friends pop in unannounced during your work hours, a new boundary could be that they only pop in after 5pm unless it was otherwise prearranged with you. Or if a loved one questions how you conduct your days (with an undertone of judgment), you can employ avoidance by answering the questions with vague responses like work is work. Or you can confront him/her and ask why they want to know. If they say they are genuinely interested in what you do, offer to send them marketing materials about your project so he/she can promote it within their network. If they scoff at this, then say, ok then I'd appreciate it if you'd stop asking how I spend each day.

Gustav Andersson, aka The Modern Nomad, dives into great detail about how his loved ones dealt with his new nomadic life in our interview with him on Nomadic Tales. He said the life shift actually brought him closer to his mom while other relationships faded away. *"Most people don't understand this lifestyle and often think I'm running away from something, but that's ok, they don't have to understand."* He also showed us acceptance is a two way street, *"Accept your friends the way they are and how they act or you don't accept them at all. Accept the way they handle this strange situation you put them in."* Gustav has made tough decisions which have served him well and lead to a happy and passion-filled life even though others don't "get it". Plus, he makes an excellent point: once you've made your decisions, don't hold expectations about how others will react. Love them for who they are, and if they don't understand what you're doing, it's ok, they don't have to. You have control of your boundaries and your decisions, therefore focus on your path and not on others' reactions of your path. Those that are meant to stay in your life will, and those relationships will strengthen. Those that are not meant to stay alongside you in your journey will fade away, and that's ok!

YOU ARE #1

"I've always been the person who takes care of everything; at home, children, and at work. It got so bad that my health declined. Work was especially rough because I was a manager and worked in a very stressful environment. I wanted to find another job, but I had worked very hard to get where I was and I didn't want to throw that effort away, so I kept at it for 15 years! Needless to say, my health continued to deteriorate and until I finally said enough is enough. I found another job that allowed me to work from home. **I decided to focus on my needs instead of everyone else's** *and it has been amazing how unbelievably happy I have become. This is something I don't think I 've ever said in my lifetime. I've always tried to be happy, but it just didn't come naturally. It only happened because I chose to take care of myself and learned to start saying no to things that other people could do for themselves."*
~ Kari-Lynn, Utah

SELF ACCEPTANCE VS. SELF IMPROVEMENT

You're an amazing individual with skills, passions, and character like no one else. Learning how to love and accept yourself just as you love an accept your closest friends and family is challenging. Even though we are the generation of the "selfie" when it comes to handling ourselves with care, we mistakenly equate such concern as selfish or arrogant.

As you encounter hurdles in your life, ask what advice you would give to your best friend or closest family member and give that advice to yourself. Allow yourself the same breaks and compassion that you give to others. **Be gentle with yourself**. Listen to your inner dialog and take note when your voice is harsh. Instead, replace it with something kind and gentle.

For example, if you say to yourself, *"You're never going to make the money you want to make."* Notice your harsh tone, and decide to say, *"That was harsh and untrue. Actually I'm on my way to financial success. I have the drive, skills, ambition, and personality to make this a huge success, and that is what I will do."* Reference the positive affirmation list for more examples of affirmations to replace your negative statements.

Once you can love and accept yourself for exactly who you are in any given moment, you will be in a fertile space for self discovery and improvement. Sounds ironic, right? Just when you are ok with exactly where you are, you're ready for growth! Life is comical sometimes.

For My Fellow LGBTQ Brothers & Sisters

You are not broken or damaged goods, you are beautiful and perfect just as you are. You have so much to be proud of, don't hide your light. Shine that rainbow across the world. The more light we pour into the world, the better and brighter it becomes for us all. When you're proud of who you are, **all** of who you are, and don't avoid conversations that "out" you, the world becomes a better place for everyone. Let those who are trapped in ignorance, fear, and hatred sleep in the bed *they* made. It's not your problem, so why should you carry it? Remember, Agreement #4- Don't take things personally- their fear, ignorance, and hateful behavior has zero to do with you and 100% to do with them. Be an ambassador for the LGBT community. People fear what they don't know, help them see there is nothing to fear by being a proud and out member of society.

In my experience, if you're comfortable with yourself and your sexuality, everyone around you will be comfortable with you as well. If you hide part of who you are in shame, it makes others uncomfortable. They don't know what they're allowed to talk about and what they must avoid. Don't create a gay elephant in the room that will slow progress for us all.

For those of you who are thinking, *"Sure, I'll bet she had a super supportive family and coming out was a breeze for her, well not for me… It's different."* Spoiler alert, aside from my sister, my family consists of ultra-conservative, right-wing fundamental Christians (was that enough adjectives?). When I came out to them, I was called a shame to the family, told I was going to hell, and compared to a baby rapist… I didn't say it would be easy, but here's my logic. I can either have an inauthentic relationship with people I love and hurt myself by hiding the wonderful person I am, or I can offer them a chance to have a true and authentic relationship with me. Sharing who you are with others is a true gift, it's up to them to accept or reject it.

Over 10 years later my family hasn't shifted their beliefs or actions, I have no regrets. I'm with an amazing woman and am proud of who I am. I treasure the numerous wonderful childhood memories and am grateful I was raised with so much love and attention, even if they dropped the ball when I turned out to be a gay adult. I give much credit to my confidence and charisma to how I was raised. The more I focus on what I'm grateful for, the less I focus on frustration, anger, or other destructive cycles.

OVERCOMING YOUR PAST
rearview mirror syndrome

What drives your choices? Are your actions intentional steps towards your goals and the best version of you or are they taken in order to avoid pain and mistakes of the past? If you are guiding your life with your rearview mirror it's not wonder you feel lost!

Did you know we are the only species who suffer more than once for a mistake? We torment ourselves over simple and complex errors repeatedly, as if we must pay a penance. This torture is self defeating and serves no purpose other than sabotaging our aspirations and lowering the ceiling on us.

At the extreme level, PTSD causes the inflicted to relive their worst experiences and fears. For others, who don't suffer from PTSD, there are triggers and soft spots that when stimulated elicit irrational responses and behaviors. For example, if a business you started went under you may be too scared to even consider another entrepreneurial venture. That's a prime example of rearview mirror syndrome. Maybe he/she has an entrepreneur's spirit and creativity but are paralyzed by fear of a repeat failure. Read ANY business book today and you'll learn that most successful business owners have a history of 1+ failed ventures.

You don't need to take my word about it:

- Before Evan Williams co-founded Twitter launched a podcasting platform that crashed and burned.
- Reid Hoffman created an online dating site called SocialNet that failed before he went on to co-found LinkedIn.
- Milton Hershey failed at three candy businesses before he started the Hershey Company which has become a household name.

FLEXIBILITY

It may take numerous attempts before you find the work-life balance and lifestyle where you will thrive. After all, you won't know if your dream-life is actually what you want until you live it. So don't punish yourself if after you give a new lifestyle a fair shake, you don't enjoy it. If you move to another country and decide it's not for you, that's ok. Welcome change into your life. If the first few doors you attempt to open don't work out it's likely because there's a much better option for you around the corner. If I hadn't hurt my back, I wouldn't have experienced the life changing move to Costa Rica, and the following nomadic lifestyle!

Life is liquid. Enjoy each minute for what it is, the present. No matter how advanced our wrestling skills, we cannot hold any given moment into submission. "It was better when…" is an example of trying to relive and hold onto something instead of appreciating the experience, learning from it, and moving forward. You don't want to base your decisions moving forward by what is in your rear view mirror. It is easy to outgrow what might have been perfect for you for the last decade. Instead, make your decisions based on how you feel now and where you're going. If your goal is to live an international life, make sure you measure each decision against that goal. If you want to work from home and control your own schedule, make your decisions accordingly.

Therefore, you must not only remain flexible, but self-aware with a system that requires you to check-in on a regular basis.

TAKING ACTION

Set an alert in your Google (or other) calendar for every week (for the first two months in a new lifestyle), then every month for the next three months, and finally every six months until the end of time to remind you to reassess how your life choices are treating you. We will dive deeper into this in the **RR- Reassess & Repeat** section.

An Introduction to saying **NO**

Overachiever, overcommitted, doormat— do these words describe you at times? In this attention-challenged society, we have normalized hectic schedules packed with tasks we don't want to do. Why and for what good? To be the perfect cookie-cutter, white-picket fence family? While I believe it's important to give back, how and when should align with *your* goals and priorities. Saying no is a key skill required in order to live your Life Another Way. You need to have full control of your calendar, scheduling blocks of time for exercise, achievement of goals, work, family time, etc. These blocks need to correspond in size with your priorities. If you're asked to volunteer during a time period that is taken or it would spread you thin thereby jeopardizing the quality of the rest of the day, say no. There will be times you will help out, and other times where it won't work. Allow yourself to say no guilt-free, with the knowledge that you are working toward your goals and your best you which will benefit everyone in your life. Saying yes when you are stretched too thin decreases your experiences across the board. The rest of your tasks will be ill performed due to fatigue, lack of focus, and potential burn out.

Plus, your refusal to say no leads to resentment. It's easy to blame the ask-ee for putting you in "this situation" when they know your plate is already full. Helping others when you should have said no, leads to agitation telling yourself, "I could be getting _____ off of my to-do list, instead I'm here doing this…" The only person you have to blame, however, is you. It's your responsibility to say no and take care of yourself. Remember, take responsibility for yourself!

SAYING NO TO THE RAT-RACE

Jen, a Wisconsin native, met and married her husband Greg in Dallas where Jen worked in commercial title insurance and Greg as the vice president for a mid-sized company. They enjoyed city living, flashy clothing, and fine dining without much concern for cost.

While money was flowing in, their energy and quality-time escaped them. Between social commitments, constant and mundane tasks like car and house maintenance, grocery shopping, and ever increasingly demanding jobs, life felt like a rat-race.

They decided they needed to live their Life Another Way and set out looking for solutions.

They researched life in Panama, Belize, Ecuador, and Costa Rica. Panama was decidedly too hot for their tastes, Belize too expensive, Ecuador too far from the U.S...and Costa Rica was too perfect to resist!

In order to make the move, the couple knew they would need to live more frugally, so they made a concerted decision to live with less. Jen elaborates, *"Even though there are little inconveniences here, they dim in comparison to living a simple life surrounded by natural beauty and wildlife. I am constantly amazed at how much I don't need to live and be happy here."*

MISTAKES

"Last night as I was sleeping, I dreamt—marvelous error!— that I had a beehive here inside my heart. And the golden bees were making white combs and sweet honey from my old failures."
~ Antonio Machado, translated by Robert Bly

In our **Pump Up Your Body** module, you'll learn that in order to build muscle you must tear it down first. As long as you provide the nutrients and rest required, it will grow stronger. The same process happens to us in our conscious and unconscious development. Life's challenges and our mistakes are the gym for our mind and soul. Each burden and mistake we make rips an old

38

part of us, breaking us down in order to build us back stronger. I'll bet you can think of a difficult time in life and link it directly to something about your personality. Who you are and how you relate to the world around you is improved because of it. Mistakes are the secret ingredient to success.

EXCUSES AND SOLUTIONS, ACT NOW!

"If you really want to do something, you'll find a WAY. If you don't, you'll find an EXCUSE." ~ Jim Rohn

My dog hurt his foot, I have too much work, it's too smokey outside from the nearby fires… There is an endless list of excuses we can conjure up to avoid doing something. In this case it was exercising. This section is the proverbial kick in the ass and a friendly slap to the face— KNOCK IT OFF! YOU KNOW BETTER!

Kids' imaginations fire from all cylinders when they try to get something, they come up with any bargaining chip available, "I'll wash the car, feed the dog, sell lemonade…" The imagination of adults fires full force when trying to come up with a reason to avoid doing something— The dishes need to be done, I need more rest in order to exercise more effectively tomorrow, I forgot my goggles, and the list goes on. The kids have it right. When you design your life in the corresponding module, you will make your goals and vision extremely clear. With those, you need to come up with every excuse and bargaining chip in your capability as to how and why you will get there.

Harness your imagination for the good and watch the life you never knew you could have become a reality. Sounds cheesy but it really can be that simple. Ok, let's address a few more common excuses.

IF I COULD AFFORD IT…

You fill in the rest of that sentence. This is one most of us have been caught using. If I could afford to travel and live in Costa Rica for the winter, I would! I've got news for you, if you restructure your life, you can afford it! You are only limited by what you think is possible and your imagination! If you own your house, you could do a house swap with homeowners in the country of your choice. Each home owner still pays his/her mortgage but you get to enjoy someone else's home in another city around the world. Renters and owners alike can save during the year for a rental abroad where your dollar stretches further. Depending on your location, after considering savings in food, alcohol, and entertainment, you may even end up on top.

"Perhaps the biggest tragedy in our lives is that freedom is possible, yet we can pass our years trapped in the same old patterns."
~ Tracy Brach, Radical Acceptance

Put your money where your mouth is. The same people who tell me they wish they could travel as much as I do dump money into multiple cars, insurance, excessive electronics, clothes, new shoes, cable TV (Why? Netflix is awesome!), eating meals out, etc. They can travel like I do (or better) by living with less overhead and simplifying their life which we will teach you how to do in the **Simple is Better** module.

After you put your money where your mouth is, lower your overhead and simplify your life, you can also address the the same excuse from the other end of the scale— Make more money. If you're working for the man, ask for a raise. If you believe your work is worth more, find someone else who will pay more. If your work isn't valued at the income you desire, it's time to apply different skills that will pay for the lifestyle that aligns with your Life Another Way. I'm biased to the attainable goal of starting your own business because I don't like answering to other people or the inspiration killer a.k.a. bureaucracy. Plus I enjoy setting my own hours and taking a vacation when I want. Learn how you can start your own business in our module titled, **Start a Business From Anywhere in the World**.

As you can see, getting to your dream life will take work and dedication, but what else is worth the effort? You can either give a half-ass effort for a mundane life or give it everything you have and live life on your terms! Why is this even a discussion? Done and done...

Remember, reshaping your life is the hardest part. Once you are living the life you designed, the upkeep is easy and a blast! Ok, now that you're psyched, let's redesign your life! Head to the next module— **Design Your Life**.

> *"It's not the years in your life that count. It's the life in your life."*
> ~ Abraham Lincoln

Designing Your Dream Life

"The master in the art of living makes little distinction between his work and his play, his labor and his leisure, his mind and his body, his information and his recreation, his love and his religion. He hardly knows which is which. He simply pursues his vision of excellence at whatever he does, leaving other to decide whether he is working or playing. To him he's always doing both." ~ James A. Michener

---

You are the architect in your life. In this course I'm going to show you how to design your life, ask the question you need to answer in order to find your sweet spot, and provide you the tools to get there. Now is the time that we replace indefinite, vague dreams with specific, detailed goals and action plans. The ability individuals have right now to deliberately design their lives and realities is greater than at any time in history.

As you brainstorm about your ideal life, make a concerted effort to remove the box you've unknowingly placed yourself in. With technology today, you have the flexibility to arrange your life exactly as you'd like it. If you don't like working for other people YOU can start your own business (learn how later in the book). If financial success is a major focus, write exactly what income you want and we'll break it down into actionable steps to get there. If you want to live in an exotic island, you can. If you want to run a nonprofit that helps animals you can. Dream big! Remember this life is based on your loves and passions, not what you're supposed to do.

LIFESTYLES AROUND THE WORLD

There are as many ways to live on this earth as there are cultures and people. You can live self-sustaining, completely off of the grid, you can roam the world nomadically staying a month in each place you pass through, you can live on a boat and sail around the world and through the tropics, live a life on an RV and have your backyard change every week, spend half of your year in the dessert and the other half in the mountains, etc. You could live in Costa Rica, Ecuador, Thailand, or Hawaii and work from your Tiki hut. Why not?

Make sure and write down your answers to all of the exercises in your journal or directly in this book. Thinking about each question won't yield results, and that is what we're about, so get your pen out.

W.S. 3.1

Answer the following questions:

Describe your average day.

_____

_____

_____

_____

_____

_____

_____

_____

_____

_____

_____

_____

_____

_____

_____

_____

Why do you live where you live? Is this something you'd like to change?

_____
_____
_____
_____
_____
_____
_____
_____
_____
_____
_____
_____
_____
_____
_____
_____
_____
_____
_____
_____

What limits have you placed on your life and behavior?

_____
_____
_____
_____
_____
_____
_____

Dipping back into the Agreements portion of the **Retrain Your Brain** course, what old agreements or self-criticisms are keeping you from growing and reaching your goals?

_____

_____

_____

_____

_____

Which of your daily activities are out-dated habits and routines that are no longer necessary for you?

_____

_____

_____

_____

_____

_____

_____

_____

_____

_____

_____

_____

_____

_____

_____

_____

_____

Do you have any behaviors that are triggers from events in your childhood or distant past that you can and should let go of / forgive and move forward from?

_____
_____
_____
_____
_____
_____
_____
_____
_____
_____
_____
_____
_____
_____
_____
_____
_____
_____
_____
_____

How do you **want** to spend your days?

_____
_____
_____
_____
_____
_____
_____

_____

_____

_____

_____

_____

_____

_____

_____

_____

_____

_____

_____

_____

_____

What do you most like to do?

_____

_____

_____

_____

_____

_____

_____

_____

_____

_____

_____

_____

_____

_____

_____

_____

_____

_____

_____

_____

_____

What kind of contribution do you want to make to the world?

_____

_____

_____

_____

_____

_____

_____

_____

_____

_____

_____

_____

_____

_____

_____

Where do you want to live if different from your current location?

_____
_____
_____
_____
_____
_____
_____
_____
_____
_____
_____
_____
_____
_____
_____
_____
_____
_____
_____
_____
_____

If you look at a question and can't decide between a few answers, write them all down.

Now, with those answers in mind let's discover what the best day in your life would look like. Once we have a good grasp of your perfect day we can work towards recreating it every single day! The more you document about your lifestyle goals the stronger the blueprint we can build to get you there.

Here's an example.

"I wake up at 9am and walk to a lovely surf spot I live near. I enjoy surfing for an hour or so with my wife, then we walk back to our beachfront bungalow and enjoy a hot shower and cup of world class coffee. Then my wife and I discuss what each of us wants to get done that day. After we're done "accomplishing" (5-6 hours) we either go Stand Up Paddle boarding, kayaking, or on a leisurely hike with our dog. Then we enjoy dinner and a card game with a few of our closest friends."

With your answers in mind, describe your perfect day

_____

_____

_____

_____

_____

_____

_____

_____

_____

_____

_____

_____

_____

_____

_____

_____

_____

_____

_____

_____

_____

_____

_____

_____

What do you need to change in your current life to open up the space for your ideal activities or that are in direct conflict with your new goals?

_____
_____
_____
_____
_____
_____
_____
_____
_____
_____
_____
_____
_____
_____
_____
_____
_____
_____
_____
_____
_____
_____
_____

Looking at your perfect day, there are likely some aspects you can start right now. Who doesn't love immediate gratification? Start introducing these "perfect moments" one by one into your life. For example, maybe your ideal life includes an after dinner walk, start this tradition now! The more things you can remove from your life that are inhibiting your goals the more room you will have in your day for those moments you've deemed perfect for you. Inspect your life for activities that are "time sucks." Was watching TV part of your perfect day? If you spend your evenings watching TV that's 5+ hours that could be spent doing something you love.

Now that you have an idea of a potential dream life, let's get more specific. Below are questions I found extremely useful from the book, <u>Click Millionaires</u> (an excellent resource if you're thinking of starting your own online business):

W.S. 3.2

Income:

✦ How much money do I want?_____

✦ How much money do I actually need each year?

_____

✦ How much would my financial situation change if I worked from home?

_____
_____
_____

If I didn't need to work at all, I would invest my time in:

✦ These 5 favorite activities:

_____
_____
_____

✦ These 5 favorite places:

_____
_____
_____

Work:Play Ratio

Work to Play ratio is a vital component when designing your life. It's a theme you will see bleed into each of our courses because without focused attention to maintain it your life will fall out of balance and your blueprint could morph from a preverbal castle in Tuscany to a sweat shop in China.

Look back at your perfect day. What was your work to play ratio? In the example provided he/she worked 5-6 hours a day (excluding weekends and vacations— but his wasn't actually mentioned). Eight hours of sleep each day yields us 16 hours to play with and 16 x 7 = 112 hours per week of time to do with as we choose. Six hours of work per weekday averages 30 hours per week or 27% of his/her time (30/112 x 100). I'd round this lifestyle to a 25:75 work to play ratio.

I have a secret for you… Working less hours doesn't mean you're less productive. In fact for me, working 5-6 hours per day is my sweet spot! I am the most productive because I'm energized and excited about my project. I avoid burnout and have plenty of time in my day to hike, SUP (stand up paddle board), and enjoy loved ones. I find that when I push myself to work after my mind and body are done it's counterproductive in a variety of ways. That doesn't mean that I don't fluctuate, I am a creature that thrives in change so there are occasions when I'm inspired for 12+ hours straight, but the next few days I usually recoup and take a break from work.

Look at your ratio. What percent do you have to play? _____ How would you like to use it? Think about your life goals / bucket list. There are things you want to accomplish that aren't part of your perfect day.

For Example:
+ Take summers off
+ Travel more
+ Drive your kids to school each day
+ Finish a degree
+ Own a dog, horse, pig, chickens, bees, etc
+ Loose weight or gain muscle
+ Join a recreation league (soccer, hockey, volleyball, basketball, etc)
+ Volunteer at the humane society, soup kitchen, red cross, etc.
+ Host a game night once a week
+ Enjoy fine dining
+ Have a 3 day weekend every week/ work 4 days a week
+ Learn Spanish

Your turn! Write some of your goals that you'd like to have or do with your play time:

_____

_____

_____

_____

_____

_____

_____

_____

_____

_____

_____

_____

_____

_____

_____

_____

"A giant pile of money isn't going to do you a fat lot of good unless you know what you want to do with your life." ~ Nora Dunn (The Professional Hobo) - an excerpt from our podcast with Nora

You're doing great! If you're brain is slowing down take a break. This module needs to be completed in a place of excitement and passion. These questions don't get asked of us often and although they seem simple, searching for the answers can be extremely draining. So be kind to yourself and take it slow. That being said, if you're ready to talk about your favorite things in life proceed on!

FAVORITES

We've already covered your perfect day and some of your bucket list goals, now let's dive into your favorite things across the board of life.

W.S. 3.3

My Favorite Things:

5 favorite hobbies

_____
_____
_____
_____
_____

5 favorite work related activities

_____
_____
_____
_____
_____

5 favorite places

_____
_____
_____

5 favorite types of projects

_____

_____

_____

_____

_____

5 favorite types of people

_____

_____

_____

_____

_____

In my life I want more of:

5 leisure activities

_____

_____

_____

_____

_____

5 work-related activities

_____

_____

_____

_____

_____

5 material objects

_____

_____

_____

_____
_____

In my life I was less of:

5 current job activities

_____
_____
_____
_____
_____

5 current personal activities

_____
_____
_____
_____
_____

5 certain people or types of people

_____
_____
_____
_____
_____

Short-term Goals:

In the next six months the 5 things I would most like to change are

_____
_____
_____
_____
_____

Long-term Goals:

In the next 24 months the 5 things I would most like to change are

_____

_____

_____

_____

_____

Drawing on the exercises you've already completed, start a detailed new brainstorming list of 20 likes and 20 dislikes about your life and work situations

LIKES	DISLIKES

LIKES	DISLIKES

Now Prioritize the list you've created. Label each like and dislike 1-10, 10 signifying the thing you like/dislike the most. Review your list. Are there any likes that are impossible (i.e. be taller)? Remove any impossibilities from you list. Now take the top ten from each side (like/dislike) creating a new list of 20 entries.

LIKES	DISLIKES

LIKES	DISLIKES

Now rank the 20 entries, 1-20 with 1 symbolizing the most important and highest priority (whether it's something you must get rid of or something you must have in your life). After you have prioritized your list 1-20, chop off the last 10 entries.

LIKES / DISLIKES

You will be left with the top ten most important lifestyle changes to implement in your new Life Another Way. Does your top 10 priority list reflect the life you would like to lead? This process and document will change. Maybe after you sleep on it you remember something that is key and should be added, or something else doesn't seem as important to you. Rearrange the list as needed.

Now let's sum it up. Review your perfect day and all of your answers for the course. With your answers fresh in mind consider:

1. What priorities are most important to you in your redesigned daily routine?

_____

_____

_____

_____

_____

_____

_____

_____

_____

_____

_____

_____

_____

_____

_____

_____

_____

_____

2. What activities, projects, or people are the most important in order for you to feel like you are succeeding in life?

_____

_____

_____

_____

_____

_____
_____
_____
_____
_____
_____
_____
_____
_____
_____
_____
_____

What you should be left with is what I like to call your Life Recipe. Write out another perfect day with this new recipe in mind. It might be the exact same as your initial take but do it again with this new mindset.

_____
_____
_____
_____
_____
_____
_____
_____
_____
_____
_____
_____
_____
_____
_____

Now that you have an idea what your Life Another Way looks like let's work on getting you there. We have a blueprint for you in our **Action Plan** module that includes SMART goals, time management, habits built for success, visualization / meditations, affirmations, managing fear, and more. I'll meet you there!

Additional Resources:

Books:
Click Millionaires

Podcasts:
Nomadic Tales
Becoming an Expat

See our downloadable visualizations at lifeanotherway.com

ACTION PLAN

We're on a roll, en route to your Life Another Way! This module is your blueprint for your new life. You will master tools like SMEAR goals, time management, habits built for success, visualization / meditations, affirmations, managing fear, and more. Let's dive in!

If you feel overwhelmed about the massive changes about to occur in your life, just remember it's as easy as 1-2-3.

1. **Retrain Your Brain**— *Make new agreements with yourself that align with your dream life.*
2. **Choose Your Custom Designed Life**— *Make your priorities and choices based on your new life design.*
3. **Take Action**— *Take a step forward every day. Utilize your goal achievement and time management skills to help in this endeavor*

You may have read about SMART goals or the new "hipper" version, CLEAR goals, but here at Life Another Way we're all about combining the best from premium concepts, so our plan is built on the foundation we dub *SMEAR*. Yes, most definitions of smear has a negative connotation, but not today! Don't forget SMEAR is also defined as a sample of material spread thinly on a microscope slide for examination. So let's examine the ultimate goal achievement strategy.

SMEAR goals

SMEAR stands for: Specific, Measurable, Emotional, Adjustable and Restrictive.

Specific— A specific goal has a much greater chance of being accomplished than a general goal. In order to make a goal specific, make sure your goal answers the 5 W's

*Who: Who is involved?

*What: What do I want to accomplish?

*Where: Identify a location.

*When: Establish a time frame.

*Why: Specific reasons, purpose or benefits of accomplishing the goal.

EXAMPLE: A general goal would be, "Get in shape." But a specific goal would say, "Join a health club and workout 3 days a week."

Measurable— Establish solid criteria for measuring progress toward each goal.

One of Tim Ferriss' paramount points in the best seller ***The 4-HR Body*** is when you measure your results you stick to your goals. More data = better results and adherence to your fitness plan. Even Nike knew that by providing a method for recording data from runs (such as heart rate, speed, average speed, time, elevation, etc.) more people would run regularly and purchase more running products because of it. When you measure your progress, you stay on track, reach your target dates, and experience the exhilaration of achievement that spurs you on to achieve your goal.

To determine if your goal is measurable, ask questions such as......

How much? How many?

How will I know when it is accomplished?

Emotional— Goals should make an emotional connection, tapping into your energy and passion.

Adjustable— Set goals with a headstrong and steadfast objective, but as new situations or information arise, give yourself permission to refine and modify your goals. Life is liquid, changing constantly, so your plans must allow flexibility otherwise they will fight the very essence of life, and I'm sure you know who will win.

Restrictive— They should be limited in scope, duration, and size

Western society has normalized goal planning in the educational setting (i.e. entrance to your desired college, studying for the SATs, MCATs, and the GRE) but it hasn't carried over into the "real world." Sure, it's common to have a 5 year plan but it often sounds like this, *"I'd like to make partner by the time I'm 30"* or *"I want to be married and have 3 kids, own a home, and make $x by 30."* We can do a lot better than this. Refer to your answers to the worksheets in the Design Your Life module. Write down what you need to accomplish in order to reach your perfect day / your newly designed life. Make sure you satisfy each section of SMEAR as they apply. If you haven't completed that module stop this course and return after it's completed.

_____

_____

_____

_____

_____

_____

_____

_____

_____

_____

_____

_____

_____

_____

_____

_____

For example, if my dream life is to live in Thailand, own and operate my business from abroad, work 15 hours a week, and enjoy a weekly massage. I could have the following immediate goals (You will set the actual due dates instead of a count):

* **Secure resident visa**—Obtain all of the necessary paperwork to file for my temporary residency visa within 30 days.

* **Sell my belongings**— Go through my belongings and determine what I will take (only that which can fit in 2 suitcases (due by the end of the week). Then, separate the remainder of my belongings into 3 piles: donate, yard sale, and sell online (due in 14 days). Then, place ads on Craigslist, eBay, and other pertinent sites for the sale of higher end or niche specific goods. If they aren't sold by _____ date then I will donate them. If I have items that I need to store, I will move them to the storage facility or friends/family's location within 21 days.

***Pick a departure date, purchase ticket**— Purchase a ticket for departure 45 days from today _____ 2016

✳**Rent or sell house (if applicable)**— Interview property management companies and select one (due by the end of the week), or select a real estate agent and place the home on the market (due by the end of the week).

✳**Learn Some Basic Thai Phrases**— Learn basic greetings and words that will facilitate travel in Thai. Download an app or language acquisition program to assist me. (due by day 40)

✳**Tax Implications**— Research tax implications of moving my business to Thailand, consult with a CPA with an international specialty (i.e. Greenback Tax Services), decide if I should maintain it's current location in the US or file in Thailand (due on day 14).

✳**International Logistics**— Research and learn about programs, apps, international communication and banking in order to run my business with ease from Thailand (due within 21 days)

✳**Income Goals**— I'd like to earn $2,000USD which based on my research will yield me the life I want in Thailand including no fewer than one massage a week. If must sell > _____ services/ product per week to accomplish this. (You should have an entire breakdown of goals and an action plan for your business which is covered in our *Start a Business From Anywhere in the World* course.

✳**Find temporary housing in Thailand**— Shop for a short-term housing solution so I have somewhere to go when I land and stay while I get my bearings. (due by day 30)

✳**Going Away Party**— Celebrate! You did it and are set to depart for your Life Another Way!Have a killer send off, and make sure and have your best means of contact available for your loved ones that attend (i.e. Skype phone number, Skye username, email, snapchat, etc. (due by day 40-43) (Learn more about international communication in our Working Remotely & Start a Business From Anywhere modules).

The above example has an aggressive timeline with just 45 days for an international move and just skims the surface. Your goals and corresponding plan might be over the span of a year. If your goal(s) are set longer than a year out, you need to break them down into smaller chunks so you can keep them on your radar and accomplish pieces each month. Otherwise, your distant goal will remain a dream you loose track of.

REWARDS

You did it! Let's celebrate! Celebrate the wins no matter how small. Throughout your calendar and built into your goals you need to select rewards for each goal achieved no matter how small. Today, after I finish writing this section I'm going to enjoy a 4 mile walk along the Deschutes River with my Great Dane! It can be very powerful to share your journey and rewards with your loved ones. After you or your significant other reaches a milestone it might call for a night on the town, a special dinner, massage, mani/pedi, or a movie!

If you don't have room in your budget it doesn't mean you can't celebrate. I'm willing to bet there are things you love that aren't expensive. A special meal at home (maybe a comfort meal that mom used to make), a favorite dessert, a sensual massage by your special someone, have some friends over for a movie or game night, watch your favorite movie in sweat pants with your favorite candy or stovetop popcorn, etc. CELEBRATE THE WINS!

HABITS

"We are what we repeatedly do. Excellence then, is not an act, but a habit."
~Aristotle

Dream Big, Act Small

Sounds a bit unproductive but stay with me. You goals should encompass the big picture, the life you designed in all it's glory. Your actions or steps toward this goal should be the minimum amount of work you need to accomplish each given day. This way the goal becomes achievable.

Routines & Habits United

When trying to introduce a new habit if you work with your routine instead of against it you can create environmental triggers to remind you to act on your new habit. For instance, if you want to snack less and exercise more you could decide to do 10 pushups every-time you open the refrigerator door. You might even save money on your electric bill! The secret sauce here is the fact you rely on contextual cues instead of willpower.

Eliminate Excessive Options

You make thousands of choices everyday. How much energy do you really want to spend deciding what you wear, and what to eat for each meal or snacks? President Obama limits his suits to just blue or grey, this way he doesn't have to make too many decisions about what he's wearing because he says, *"…I have too many other decisions to make."* If you want to maintain long term discipline, it's best to routinize mundane aspects of your life so that you make fewer decisions.

Visualize the End Game & the Route to it

While visualization is powerful, if you also visualize the process required to obtain your goal it's power multiplies. For example, if your end-game is a tone and muscular body with 10% body fat, instead of visualizing your body in pristine condition, also visualize working out in the gym each day, sweating and enjoying the labor of love for your body. This not only reduces any anxiety you may have about achieving your goals, it helps focus your attention on the steps required to reach your goal.

Eliminate *"ah-screw-its"*

It's January 5th, you made a New Year resolution to go to the gym 3x a week and yet you're in bed when you should be half way through your workout. Why? Did you feel the warm comfort of your bed and say, *"Ah-screw-it"*? Then when your adherence streak was over did you just give up? Why are we so quick to abandon new habits? There are specific road blocks between us and our goals. The more accurate we are in determining where the roadblocks are the better our chances at adherence to our new habits and goal achievement.

For example, Author and speaker Ramit Sethi explained how he improve his gym attendance by over 300%,

"When I sat down to analyze why I wasn't going to the gym, I realized: my closet was in another room. That meant I had to walk out in the cold [to] put on my clothes. It was easier to just stay in bed. Once I realized this, I folded my clothes and shoes the night before. When I woke up the next morning, I would roll over and see my gym clothes sitting on the floor. The result? My gym attendance soared by over 300%."

73

HABITS RELATING TO YOUR ATTITUDE & SELF-COMPASSION

Leo Babauta is the creator of one of the world's most popular blog, <u>Zen Habits</u>. Leo shares how small tweaks to your habits can result in drastic lifestyle transformations. His articles are spectacularly simple, short, and are focused on self-love and compassion. He reminds us to live in the present moment and when we're harsh or feeling frustrated with our performance in life to remember three things:

1. Be aware when you're feeling angry or frustrated with yourself.
2. Be compassionate with yourself, providing the same comfort you'd give a friend in the same circumstance.
3. Change your focus on what you haven't done to what you have done

"The story so far has been: you aren't good at X. (Whatever X is.) And so we feel bad about not being good at X. Let's turn from the self we haven't been, to the self we have been... Now turn to the present moment: in this moment, what are you like? What about yourself, and the moment that you're in, can you be grateful for? What is great about yourself, and the present moment, right now?"
~ Leo Babauta

Having a predominately grateful take on your life, yourself, and your circumstance is a habit worth developing. Small tweaks on how you view each circumstance and each outcome will lead you to become a powerfully positive person. One that people will gravitate towards and one that opens doors.

Speaking of habits, lets dive into how to set up everyday for success.

THE MIRACLE MORNING
~ Created by Hal Elrod

Hal coined the expression "The Miracle Morning" after his new morning routine changed his life so dramatically he felt like it was a miracle. His income more than doubled in just four months (he owned his own business), he got into shape, his energy level and attitude drastically improved from a depression he describes as his rock bottom. I find the name a bit corny, but agree with the power of an effective morning routine.

Hal was looking for a morning routine that could help him climb out of his depression, so he googled successful morning routines. He found six major activities: journaling, meditation, exercise, visualizations, affirmations, and reading. Instead of choosing one or two activities to incorporate in his morning he chose to do 10 minutes of each one!

I'm not prescribing the same practice until the end of time, but I am asking for a valiant attempt. Wake up one hour earlier so you can squeeze this hour long routine in unencumbered. After trying it out for one week assess which activities you look forward to, which feel like they empower you the most, and then decide if there are others that are not adding value to your life. Remove the deadbeat activities (if there are any) and think of any activities you'd like to add to your morning day. Continue to experiment with *your* miracle morning until it really does feel miraculous.

While I've NEVER been a morning person. I am really enjoying waking up earlier and starting my day between 6:00am — 6:30am so my work is complete around 1pm — 2 pm. Then I'm free to enjoy a hike, kayak, or SUP (stand up paddle-board) outing. It's a great reward for me. Plus I've noticed a remarkable increase in productivity and energy! There is something special about being awake before everyone else. It's like I'm working incognito. My miracle morning also incorporates motivating and educational podcasts.

THE BULLETPROOF LIFE MANAGEMENT SYSTEM

      I like to call time management "life" management because that's what time is, your life. If you don't have a proper and productive life management system then it will be very difficult to do your best. Every individual's productivity has a unique set of variables. Some are most productive in the morning, others are creative creatures of the night. I used to call myself a strong mid-afternoon kind of gal. My creative and inspirational juices flow best after mid-day, however, if I can't wrap up my work before eight or so then I have trouble sleeping because I'm still in high productivity mode, and for me it's hard to turn off. I compare it to a high speed bike. It takes awhile and a lot of effort to really get going, but once I'm going I'm really in the zone. Which is why I don't like interruptions (I'd have to start the bike all over again). The other drawback is it's hard to stop. This means that I need to stop well before bedtime otherwise my creative juices keep me up all night. Now that I'm enjoying "miracle mornings" (you'll learn about this below) and work much earlier, starting at 6am I'm discovering I'm very productive as long as I begin work much before 8am.

      When are you most productive? Think back to your work day and when you have had the best breakthroughs. Make a note here about your brain's primetime.

_____
_____
_____
_____

Now that you know when your most productive hours are you can assign the tasks that need the most brainwork to those time slots. Which brings us to scheduling your time/life.

SCHEDULING YOUR TIME

There are a variety of ways to schedule out your time. You can use a digital calendar like Google, iCalendar, or Outlook, an application like Asana, a poster-board, whiteboard, desk calendar, or a planner. Experiment with a few different systems until you find one you can stick to. Compliance, flexibility, and ease of use are the most important factors. Regardless of which calendar method you use, make sure you have your core 5 priorities (from your *Design Your Life* course) handy in a place you can see while scheduling out your week and/or month.

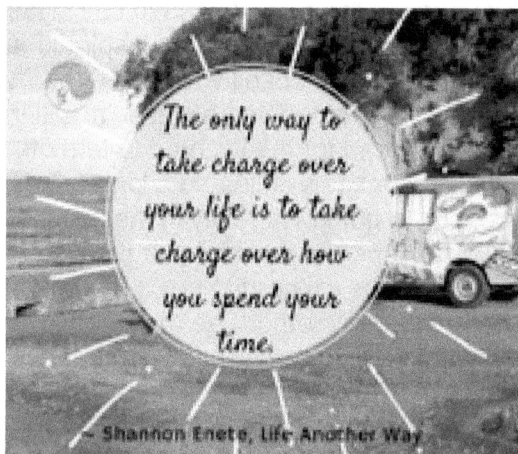

The only way to take charge over your life is to take charge over how you spend your time.

- Shannon Enete, Life Another Way

The only way to take charge over your life is to take charge over how you spend your time. In addition to your 5 core priorities also reference your ideal work:play ratio. If your ratio is 35:65 your calendar should be agreeable. Maybe 35:65 work:play ratio is a goal of yours that you've scheduled to accomplish in four months.

78

If you're currently looking at a 70:30 work:play ratio then you will need to adjust by 35%, divide that by four and you have almost 9% of change needed each month to meet your goal. We talk considerably about work:play ratios in the **Design Your Life** course but just to refresh your mind it's what percentage of time do you spend on work versus play.

Provided that you sleep 8 hours each night you're left with 16 hours per day to do with as you'd like. That's 112 hours per week! If you work from home (no commute) and strictly limit your work to 40 hours a week, your work ratio = 40/112= 36, now subtract that from 100% = 64. So the work:play ratio would be 36:64. This is with no emails or phone calls taken outside of your 40 hours and the rest of your time is spent in relaxation, recreation, and general enjoyment. Realistically, unless you have a maid you will need to factor in the hours of house maintenance, cooking meals, errands, and other required non-recreational activities on the work side of your ratio. This is an equation you need to do after scheduling each week. Make certain it adheres to your predetermined work:play ratio or goals.

My favorite method of time management is assigning blocks of time to categories of tasks. For example, I might have 2 hours on Mondays assigned to marketing for one of my businesses, 2 hours on Tuesday for content creation, 1 hour of networking on Wednesday, 3 hours on Monday, Wednesday, & Friday evening for socializing with friends, 1 hour everyday reserved for exercise, etc. Using category blocks simplifies my scheduling process, is easy to adhere to and allows me the flexibility I need.

I simply spend the last 20 minutes of my workday to review tomorrow's schedule. If tomorrow has 2 hours of marketing scheduled then I look at my marketing tasks or to-dos on Asana (I keep all of my to-do lists organized using asana.com, it's free and wonderful) and schedule the ones I find most important due tomorrow. That way when I start my day tomorrow I can dive right into what needs to be accomplished. Research shows your productivity greatly increases by spending the end of one work day planning the work needed to be completed the following work day. This system allows me the flexibility I need to run my businesses in a way that is easy to measure time spent. This is super handy when determining your return on investment (ROI) which we'll talk about in our **Start a Business From Anywhere** module.

NO MULTITASKING
Multi-tasking = Half Ass-ing

"If you chase two rabbits you will not catch either one" Russian Proverb

---

This course is all about taking action. You might think if you can multitask you get more done resulting in more action! In most cases that's not how it works. Let me explain. Until recently, multitasking has been all the rage, and for some it still is. I remember when Apple added multi-tasking to it's mobile devices so that we could bounce from one application to another with ease and speed. While technology is getting faster and faster our attention span is conversely becoming shorter and shorter. Coincidence? I think not.

IT'S PLACE

Multitasking does have a place. When you, as a mom or dad, is getting ready for work in the morning while simultaneously feeding your children or packing their lunch, plus you receive an early phone call you certainly have your hands full. The morning "send-off" is a hectic time and while some of the chaos can be solved through planning and preparation the night before there will always be surprises or extra tasks we couldn't have planned for.

As a paramedic I multitasked on every response. Shortly after walking into a residence I would listen to my patient and the conversation my partner had with the family/witness simultaneously to gain a clearer picture of the events. I'd also communicate with my team and the patient while starting an IV, breathing treatment, EKG, or other necessary intervention. In an emergency environment where time is literally the difference between life and death multitasking makes sense.

HALF *ASS-ING*

"I'm excellent at multitasking" has been written on countless resumes. It may make sense for some positions but for many you might as well write "I give only a fraction of my attention to many things at the same time" or "I half ass many tasks simultaneously." Think about what multitasking is: *"The performance of multiple tasks at one time." ~* Merriam-Webster. If you're busy performing numerous tasks at once each of those tasks gets a tiny percentage of your energy or attention. Whereas if you completed each task one at a time they would be completed with near 100% of your attention. Not only will your work show the difference but we're just now learning that multitasking is no faster in most instances because our concentration is broken our production is sluggish.

The take home message here is pick a task and do it well, then move onto the next important task. Don't allow pop ups or alerts to redirect your focus. Be the master of your mind, focus, and attention so you can live intentionally with each moment.

ALERTS
(This section is for those who are smart phone users and who enjoy social media)

Alerts have gotten out of hand. Your phone can buzz, beep, or chirp for practically any reason. If you have a smart phone and have downloaded a handful of social media applications I'm going to ask that you go into your settings then to notifications and turn them off. Doing this allows you to have the power and control as to when you will allocate time to peruse each application. If you allow the app to rule your attention you will end up checking your email every few minutes instead of once or twice daily, and will be glued to Facebook. These apps are designed to be addictive, add the notifications and you're a goner. Say goodbye to the control over your time and priorities. Do you really think that checking your Facebook twice a day instead of 100-200 times daily you'll miss out on something? You won't. Plus, by taking back control of when you assign time to social media you gain the most important commodity there is, time.

MANAGING FEAR & ANXIETY

"Fear, to a great extent, is born of a story we tell ourselves" ~ Cheryl Strayed

---

In order to make the changes necessary to live your Life Another Way you must be able to venture out of your comfort zone. To move outside your comfort zone, you have to manage fear. Anxiety and fear are critical components of humanity. 2.4 million Americans will experience a panic disorder this year and 9.1 million Americans already have an anxiety disorder. However, 100% of humans experience fear and anxiety. Let's dive into how to change your focus to decrease your fear, recognize triggers, and manage your feelings in the moment.

REFOCUS

Stop consuming yourself with what could go wrong, and set your eyes and mind on what could go right. What are you so worried about anyway? You might try a new way of living and decide it's not for you, but would you regret trying? If you lay stagnant and wait on "some day" I can guarantee you will be regretful! It's always better to try and fail then fail to try.

"Failure is simply a brief stop in route to success,
so KEEP DRIVING"
~ Shannon Enete

To learn more about how to refocus your mind so that you experience less fear and anxiety refer to the **Retrain Your Brain** Course.

What fears are keeping you from living the life you want? Take the time to identify them and write them below or in your journal.

W.S. 1.3

LIST YOUR FEARS KEEPING YOU FROM LIVING YOUR LIFE ANOTHER WAY

_____

_____

_____

_____

_____

_____

_____

_____

_____

_____

_____

_____

_____

_____

_____

_____

_____

_____

_____

_____

_____

_____

_____

_____

_____

_____

_____

_____

_____

_____

_____

_____

_____

_____

_____

"Don't let the fear of the time it will take to accomplish something stand in the way of your doing it. The time will pass anyway; we might just as well put that passing time to the best possible use."
~ Earl Nightingale

Identifying your fear is the first step to managing it. I don't say conquer because fear is one of the several natural emotions we have that shouldn't be judged as good or bad. Having a healthy acknowledgement of your fear and how to handle it removes it's power and potentially paralyzing influence on your decisions and life.

Visit Nomadic Tales Podcast Excerpt on Fear
(at the 30 min marker we talk extensively about fear)

The way to feel free alongside fear is through acceptance of it. Not only are we aware, but we aren't fighting it, we don't judge ourselves, our emotions, or pull away from them. Instead we invite them in as if they were dinner guests. One of life's paradoxes is that once you are truly comfortable with your fear and are not concerned about when it will depart is often the exact moment it moves on. Yup, life has a sense of humor.

86

TRIGGERS

Most people have specific events or combination of events that lead to stress, fear, and/or anxiety. Learning your triggers is well worth the work. Once you can identify what sends you into a panic or paralyzing fear you can apply a well timed coping method to redirect your path. For example, Matt from Salt Lake City says his anxiety is triggered when he has to take an exam in college, or when he thinks a friend or family member is mad at him. 9/10 times he scores an A on his exams yet he worries he won't have enough time to study or he won't perform well on the exam. When it comes to friends he worries that he has done something wrong and they are mad at him. Since Matt has the awareness that these events trigger his anxiety he can plan ahead and incorporate his best coping methods. Once his studies are complete the night before an exam he can listen to a guided meditation and visualize acing the test. Then on the morning of his exam he can wake up early for a "miracle morning" and incorporate outdoor exercise with a healthy dose of fresh air. While sitting in the class waiting for the exam to be passed out he can take a few deep breaths and smile stating to himself, "I'm going to rock this exam!"

PEACEFUL EATING

Eating a diet based on whole foods with carefully selected proteins and plenty of leafy greens will provide your body the phytonutrients you need to help reduce anxiety. Don't skip breakfast! More people with anxious disorders skip breakfast. Eggs are a great way to start the day since they are nature's top source of choline. Those with low levels of choline are often shown to have increased anxiety. Learn more about a healthy diet, phytonutrients, and glycemic load in our *Fuel Your Body* course.*

Superfoods for Anxiety: Blueberries, almonds, chocolate (60+% cacao),

Avoid: fried foods, unrefined sugars, alcohol, and high glycemic carbs. These foods wreck havoc on your hormones and neurotransmitters throwing your moods.

Supplements

Chamomile— Did you know that compounds in chamomile finds to the same brain receptors as drugs like valium?

L-theanine (or green tea)— Research shows that this amino acid in green tea keeps your heart rate and blood pressure down, and a few studies show that high doses (200mg) actually decreases anxiety. This dose requires 5-20 cups of green tea, or a supplement.

Lavender— add a few drops of this essential oil to your bath or simply take a few long whiffs to enjoy the calming effects of the herb.

Maca Root— add the powder to your food or beverages for more phytonutrients than nearly any other fruit or vegetable. It's very high in magnesium and iron both very important in the management of stress.

Kava & Valerian Root— Both of these herbs are strong depressants. If you need something to deeply relax you either of these roots will do. They will likely cause drowsiness so are best used to aid with sleep.

* I am not a physician, consult your doctor about any major diet changes or supplements.

REACH OUT

"Reach out. One of the inherent risks of attempting to "manage" fear and stress is that it causes you to become more internally than externally focused. You know that downward spiral as well as I do. So don't give in to it -- reach out. I call my sister, my mother, a friend, someone who's going through a harder time than me. I send a loving note to someone who least expects it. It makes me feel stronger, more capable, more open. And there's a beautiful boomerang effect: You send some loving, positive energy out into the world, and it comes speeding back to you, just when you need it most." ~ Terri Trespicio

Fear, at its worst, can't do the damage that I can and have done to myself.

ACTION PLAN SUM UP

Live a flexibility life with the intention to constantly reshape your goals as your passions and life redirect you. Create measurable SMEAR goals that align with your perfect day and a path towards the best you. While it's important to walk towards you goal with small steps every day, make sure you're not forgetting about the tasks at hand in the present moment.

Celebrate each win on your road to better-ness. Build in rewards and treats that correspond with goal achievement.

As you redesign your life and schedule out your time make sure you uphold the work:play ratio that you laid out in your perfect day, otherwise, you miss the mark completely and could be on the road to burnout once again.

Don't let fear lead your decisions, instead acquaint yourself with each fear. Don't fight them. Invite them in for dinner, explore the depths of each fear. The more you understand your fear the less power it holds. Fear will always be part of your life, don't fight it, learn about it.

Following this ACTION PLAN yields a proactive life. We are groomed to live reactive lives, driven by the actions of those we care about or are envious of. As we reshape what we believe to be true about ourselves, reallocate our time to tasks we have discovered most important to us, our best-selves and dream-life will know no bounds. Your life is no longer be lead by fear or jealously, leaving room to live a life inspired by your heart.

Additional Resources:

Books:
Click Millionaires
Help and Hope for Your Nerves
7 Habits of Highly Effective People
The Power of Habit: Why We Do What We Do in Life and Business
The One Thing: the Surprisingly Simple Truth Behind Extraordinary Results

Podcasts:
Nomadic Tales- Crossing the Pacific- The Wet Nomad
Anxiety Slayer
The Anxiety Guru Show

BURNOUT

Merriam-Webster Definition: *"Exhaustion of physical or emotional strength or motivation usually as a result of prolonged stress or frustration."*

Wikipedia relates it specifically to work, *"Burnout is a psychological term that refers to long-term exhaustion and diminished interest in work. Burnout has been assumed to result from chronic occupational stress (e.g., work overload)."* It later compares the signs and symptoms of burnout to clinical depression, showing a striking similarity.

Burnout is an epidemic in the United States, and is one of the most untreated problems in our society. Since economic values are placed ahead of human values I don't foresee a decline of burnout in our society anytime soon. I do however, plan to cure it from our Life Another Way community, *the outlaws*. If burnout isn't an ailment you suffer from proceed on to the next module, **Spectacularly Simple**.

While society has groomed you to work harder, longer, and for less I will help reprogram you to do what you love, use your creativity alongside technology, in order to avoid burnout, stay healthy and happy, and to recognize the signs when a change or shift is necessary.

CAUSES

Burnout occurs when you feel overwhelmed and are unable to meet demands over a span of time. As the stress continues, you begin to lose the interest or motivation that led you to take on a certain role or project in the first place. Your passion and love for a cause are shadowed by the overwhelming stress of the project. What once was fun and important becomes a barrier to happiness and health in your life.

Your work environment or lifestyle can cause burnout.

Work-Related Causes

- A feeling of little or no control over your work
- Lack of recognition or appreciation
- Unclear or demanding expectations
- Brainless work
- A chaotic or high-pressure work environment

Lifestyle Causes

- Work: Play balance is tilted towards all work and very little play
- Lack of socializing, and cultivating close supportive friendships
- Not taking time out to relax and recharge
- Having too many expectations of from too many people close to you
- Saying yes when you should have said no, taking on too many responsibilities
- Lack of sleep

Based on our personality, some have a higher risk of burnout. If the traits below sound familiar take extra care to look for the signs of burnout and give yourself the care and treatment needed to avoid a burnout induced depression.

Personality Traits with Higher Risk

- Perfectionists
- Pessimistic view of yourself and the world
- The need to be in control, reluctant to delegate
- Type A, high achieving personality

SIGNS AND SYMPTOMS

When you're burnout your productivity drops dramatically, your energy is nil, leaving you feeling helpless, hopeless, cynical, and resentful. Eventually, you may feel empty with nothing more to give.

We all have "off" days where we feel bored, overwhelmed, or discouraged. So how does one determine if they are having a few "off" days in a row or are headed down the path of burnout?

Warning! Burnout Ahead if:

- Every day is a bad day.
- You are completely discouraged about your home and work life.
- You're exhausted all the time and struggle to get out of bed for work.
- Frequent headaches, back pain, muscle aches
- Much of your day is spent on tasks you find dull or overwhelming.
- You feel as if nothing you do makes a difference or is appreciated.
- You notice long-term changes to your body (i.e. weight loss or gain and/or chronic pain) and are more vulnerable to illnesses like colds and flu.
- Sense of failure, self-doubt, self-defeated
- Loss of motivation
- Increasingly negative outlook on life and your circumstances
- Procrastination
- Isolating yourself

PREVENTION AND TREATMENT

Burnout only gets worse if you ignore it. Now that you know what it looks like let's take a look at how to prevent and treat it. Much of burnout is due to an imbalance in your life, a shift in your work:play ratio, an increase in demands or stress, a shift in

93

your mental challenges or appreciation of your talents. It's no surprise that in order to correct your path you need to restore balance and health to your life.

PREVENTION

The Miracle Morning— start your day off right! It's not only great for personal and financial development it's a way to reignite the fire inside, refocus your efforts and remind you why you're doing what you're doing. Plus, if you're headed down the wrong path, the miracle morning helps bring that awareness to you, along with the confidence needed to change course.

Premium Octane For Your Body, Mind, & Soul— It's amazing how much better you feel when you drink enough of water (.5-1 ounce per pound you weigh, i.e if you weigh 200 LBS you should drink between 100-200 ounces per day), eat right, exercise regularly, and enjoy quality sleep. This tip alone can be the difference from burnout or depression and a successful happy life.

Say No— Don't overextend yourself. As we mentioned earlier saying no allows you to be the best you at the tasks that are most important to you.

Disconnect— Enjoy some time out from technology everyday! Close your laptop, silence or turn off your phone, and enjoy an alert-free moment. This could be a good time to take a walk around the block or to your favorite park. Enjoy some light stretching. Breath in the fresh air, and bask in the sun. After all, you need at least 10 minutes of sun each day for an adequate dose of Vitamin D.

Feed Your Creativity— Feeding your creativity is kryptonite to burnout. Make sure your hobbies or creative projects are fun and stress-free.

Allstar Coping Methods— We have a lot more control over our stress than you might think. Learning how to manage and address stress not only helps you gain balance in your life, and keep burnout at bay, it will help every aspect of your life: relationships, work, play, travel, and dealing with change, just to name a few!

TREATMENT

When you're experiencing full-blown burnout it's going to take time and gentle treatment to recover. The #1 rule is be kind to yourself! Give yourself time to rest, reflect, and heal. This means, SLOW DOWN, cut back on your responsibilities wherever possible. Find more time with your close friends and family, those who are positive and believe in you and your abilities. Open up and talk to those in your inner circle about what you're going through. Tell them you're not looking for solutions, you just need to vent.

From a place of support analyze your life. Write down what is working and what is not. Retake the *Design Your Life* course so you can come up with a plan that will lead to a life balanced on what is important to you now which will simultaneously dump the deadweight tasks that serve as anchors to your happiness.

Once you have a grasp over what your redesigned life looks like revisit this course to implement it. This is the phase where you'll be ready to implement changes to your routine (like the miracle morning) and your health which will close season for burnout.

SPECTACULARLY SIMPLE

It's amazing what we convince ourselves we need in order to be happy. In many occasions it's learning to live with less provides the freedom conducive for happiness. That being said, this isn't the section where I tell you if you want to keep your stuff you're evil. I just want to open your eyes to various options and what each route provide you. Everyone has a different set of "must haves." For instance, I've learned I don't enjoy life in a tropical environment without air conditioning. I know I'll be miserable, so I happily pay the extra money for a rental that is equipped with AC and the corresponding electric bill.

Myth Bust:

Having a crazy, hectic, life doesn't make you more important or your life more fulfilled, it just distracts you from what is real and from the present moment.

Life is simple. Society is complicated. So let's see how we can merge the two into a happy medium where we blend our basic needs with a few extras we enjoy, without making everything so complicated.

Have you ever looked around at home and just felt completely overwhelmed with things to do? There is work, cleaning, organizing, cooking, redecorating, laundry, and you still haven't cleaned out the garage or the basement, and the list goes on!

Our society as become accustomed to accumulation of so many status symbols that we can no longer manage them. We've surrounded ourselves with an overabundance of stuff that causes us more grief, maintenance and expense than they're worth. We buy bigger and better things only to later feel overwhelmed by debt and dissatisfaction. This tendency doesn't only empty out our wallet, it occupies our time and energy.

Our abundant belongings are anchors both physically and mentally.

The generation who grew up during The Great Depression taught the next generation a valuable lesson: you never know when hardship might strike, so save everything for a rainy day. The era of hoarding began. Nothing could be thrown out if it could possibly serve a purpose someday in some potential crisis. It's perfectly understandable how this mentality began.

But a booming economy and an increasingly materialistic society did not coincide with this lesson from the previous generation. As people made more money, they were told to spend it on more things. Owning more stuff became a symbol of status: the bigger house, the newer car, the latest technology. The more things you had, the more important you were. But, also, don't throw anything away because you never know when that rainy day might come. So we bought bigger homes to accommodate our need for storage space to fill with all of our stuff.

Does any of this sound familiar?

Here's the catch: Buying more stuff does not buy your happiness. Surrounding yourself with things does not surround you with love. Filling a home with the latest technology does not offer you fulfillment.

That probably sounds familiar if you're seeking to live your life another way. Simplifying your life entails more than changing your physical catalog. Simplifying your life also means minimizing your activities in your schedule. Being busy to be busy, and packing your calendar only serves to create chaos in your life. Living life based on your to-do list does not offer fulfillment, it offers stress.

Learning to say "no" when an invitation arrives is just as important as clearing out the clutter. Learning to minimize your schedule is just as important as minimizing the amount of stuff stored in your home.

Simplifying your life is easier said than done for most people. It can be incredibly overwhelming to evaluate your whole life and to minimize what stays in it. It can be heart wrenching to throw away the kids' old school projects and drawings; it can be challenging to say no to gatherings and invitations.

A simplified schedule provides the time you need to pursue your passions and to create your own happiness. It provides you the option to live intentionally prioritizing what's important to you. A simplified home provides the space you need to grow and to evolve.

A simplified life isn't a stark existence where only the bare necessities are excepted. Keep your favorite electronics and book those massages! However, whatever and whoever you surround yourself with, make certain that each activity, each item, and each person has been carefully selected because of the positive impact it has on your life.

A simplified life is still a full life. It is full of love, joy, happiness, pleasure, fulfillment, achievement, satisfaction, and more. Simplify your life by actively choosing to fill it with these intangible things, rather than all those other physical things you forgot you even had in boxes stored in your basement.

Here are a few actionable tips you can start working on right away to simplify your life:

1. Open up your closet and your dresser and really look at all your clothes. Do you wear them all regularly? If you haven't worn it in a few weeks (unless it's seasonal), it's time to let it go.

a. Donate the clothes you don't wear to someone who may need them. Or sell them in a yard sale! But don't keep them piling up at home. Be honest with yourself: if you won't wear it, don't keep it.

b. Don't use the old "I might fit into it again someday" excuse. If you don't use it now, don't hold onto it. If you're working hard at losing weight and getting fit, then you can always reward yourself with a new pair of jeans to fit your new size. Those old ones can go to a new home.

2. Take a look at your calendar. Do you have an activity every single day? Do all of those activities make you happy?

a. If you have something on the calendar that you are dreading, think about whether or not you really need to go. If you absolutely do need to attend, go for the amount of time necessary and go with a positive attitude.

b.If you have events on the calendar that don't bring you joy, cross them out. If your kids are running from one activity to the next, ask them what they love to do most and stick to it. A blank day on the calendar grants you and your family time to get creative and to see where your hearts and minds take you!

c.If you truly cannot eliminate items from your calendar, then it's time to add more appointments. This isn't something to pencil in; use a pen. Ready? Schedule unplugged time for yourself. Write it in ink. Whatever you do in that time is up to you! Read a book, or meditate, or take a walk…just do something that provides quiet time alone for your mind to stretch. Put away the electronics and grant yourself the time you need to simply be. Eventually, if you schedule enough of this time into your busy calendar, you won't need to write it down anymore. You'll make sure you take the time you need whenever you need it. Simplicity!

3. Let's tackle all that stuff you have stored throughout your home. Do you have boxes of photos, greeting cards, books, drawings; boxes of "memories" stored in the basement and the attic and the

garage? It's time to go through them. ALL of them. This isn't an easy task! This will be time-consuming and exhausting. Here's how we are going to tackle this project.

a. Step one: If you like handwriting notes, grab an empty journal and a pen. Otherwise, grab the laptop.

b. Step two: Start somewhere. Open up a box, any box. Start there. It can be overwhelming to look at all you've accumulated over time, but you'll accomplish nothing if you don't just start somewhere. Even if you're young and haven't lived in the same house for decades, you've still accumulated extra stuff. Go through it now.

c. Step three: Slowly, painstakingly, go through every item you have stored. If it evokes a memory, write it down. Write down the stories and the people and the feelings. And once it's written down, let go of the physical object. Throw away the cards and the school projects; donate or sell the old clothes, toys, and books. If it's a photo, glue it into the journal with the story or scan it into your computer and add it into your document. Having boxes of photos with no caption or story won't help your loved ones to identify or care about them years later. But for your family to have memory books filled with short stories and tales from all the memories evoked will be a treasure.

d. Step four: Keep going. You started and you probably have quite a ways to go. But keep going. Once you have gone through all of the boxes and the bins and the bags, you will be left with plentiful memories for your family and friends to enjoy. And to enjoy those memories, they won't have to dig through all of that stuff. Plus, your home will be cleared of the clutter that has served as anchors holding you back. So keep going!

4. Reassess and Reevaluate. Do this constantly! Things and stuff will accumulate again, and activities will fill up the calendar again, and the anchors will return. It's up to you to continuously review your life and to decide what to change. Add and subtract items and people from your life. Your life is liquid; just go with the flow and don't throw down too many anchors.

WORKING REMOTELY

Travel-size your job, or get a one that is already travel-sized

---

Working remotely comes with many names: telework, telecommute, work from home, location independent...and the list goes on. They all mean is the same thing: more freedom. Telecommuting has increased by 80% from 2005 to 2012.

Freeing up your office location means you can literally work from anywhere in the world. Technology has improved to the point that you can literally work from the the other side of the world, or your favorite tropical island and still stay connected to your clients, market, or customers.

Your employer may require you to be available during the usual work hours of a specific time zone and while that might translate into a 5am-1pm workday, but when you're off at 1pm, think of all that daylight time you have to explore the area you're traveling through! Or maybe your time zone will require you to work 2pm-10pm, which would allow you to sleep in and enjoy a leisurely breakfast before heading out to see what the world has to offer. Oftentimes when you work remotely you're granted the freedom to create your own schedule. Which is ideal in order to compliment your newly designed life.

Who should work remotely?

There's a certain breed of person who can pull this off successfully. Primarily, you must be self-motivated. If you're the guy/gal that slacks off when the boss is gone and you need direction in order to be productive this isn't for you. If you're the type who knows what has to get done and prefers to be left to it, you'll do nicely in a remote work environment.

Discipline and time management are required in order to work remotely. You have to be able to segregate social media for work and social media for personal use.

Finally, to be successful working remotely, you must love what you do. This is the case with all work. If you hate your job day in and day out, now is the time to change your life. Whatever your skill set, you can find an alternative solution. You have to. If you stay in a job you loathe, you are wasting precious moments.

So what can you do?

Change your life.

Investigate if remote work is an option for you in your current job? If so, start now. Whatever has been holding you back, take a step forward toward achieving your goals. You might surprise yourself! Be the employee they don't want to lose and will do anything to keep.

How to convince your boss to let you work remotely

Working remotely has benefits for both you and your employer. If your employer is hesitant to allow you to work remotely, employ the following plan:

Ask your boss for a 10 minute meeting at his earliest convenience. Prepare a powerpoint or video presentation where you address his/her concerns and prove why remote work is a win-win for you and your boss. Restrict your presentation to 5 key slides:

1. Employees who work from home take fewer personal and sick days than employees in an office.
   - Less stress = less sickness
   - More time for exercise (due to the elimination of a commute)
   - Decreased exposure to germs around the office (flu season won't take everyone out at once)

2. Remote workers are proven to be more productive than their office dwelling counterparts.

3. Higher morale and employee retention

4. More money in the _____(company's) pocket due to:
   - Decreased office space needs
   - Saving in utilities
   - Less hardware requirements, and IT upkeep
   - Less phone lines and office equipment required for the same amount of work
   - You can advertise your company as more environmentally friendly through the use of remote workers (less utilities and less people commuting to work)

5. In order to be considered for remote work an employee must: (Create a list of requirements needed in order for an employee to work remotely). Treat it like a promotion, a reward for superior performance. For example:
   - Have worked for at least 1 year with the company
   - Have zero written or verbal warnings (empty file)
   - Have access to a computer less than ___ years old, or with certain specs
   - _____ Minimum internet speed required
   - Apply for a remote work trial that can be approved or denied by management
   - Demonstrate their ability for self-directed work with a **one-month trial period** where the employee works from home on Tuesdays and Thursdays

Hopefully, you've peaked his/her curiosity. At the end of the presentation hand your boss a **Plan of Action** that you've created to address further concerns and to show you mean business. You must demonstrate the initiative required to be an excellent remote worker from the get-go. You can do this by creating a plan that includes: what technology you will be using at home (Type of computer, internet speed, programs/software, etc.), that you have a home office clear from distractions, share the current research proving the benefits and drawbacks of telecommuting, how you plan to avoid potential problems or communication breakdowns, and how you will safeguard proprietary information.

If at this point you are still shot down, I would capitalize on the trial period. Ask him what day of the week would be best to for a trial run. Make sure and deliver a high-visibility important project at the end of your day at home. Make it a show-stopper!

LIFE HACKS FOR REMOTE WORKERS

There are a variety of programs, apps, habits, and practices that can smooth your transition into the telecommuting life.

Reward yourself.

If you complete a task early, reward yourself. Whether it's with a fun break activity or a special night out on the town, do something that makes you smile. Reward systems are used in workplaces everywhere, so there's no need to cut it out just because you're not in a traditional office environment.

Find balance.

It's easy to lose sight of your schedule and the line between work and home life can become blurred if you aren't careful. To avoid this you must create a work/life balance that clearly delineates your focus time and your personal time. If you're required to work a certain number of hours in a day, make sure you log your focused work hours and don't let your work leak into your time off.

More often than not the trouble isn't getting the remote worker to log enough hours due to lack of supervision it's getting them to stop working. Remote workers often work many more hours than their office counterparts, partly due to the fact that their office is in their home. There is no clear line when work ends and their time off begins since they don't have to "leave work," unless they work hard to create one. Which is why it's important to create these boundaries in order to prevent burnout.

Utilize scheduling tools and resources.
Explore these resources and see what works best for you.

RescueTime: This online resource tracks your productivity by measuring where you spend time on your computer. Once you download it, you can customize which websites and applications count as being productive, neutral, or unproductive. For example, www.lifeanotherway.com is considered to be a very productive website, while 9gag.com is considered to be very unproductive. If you track your computer activity with this app, you'll likely notice some interesting trends in your workday performance. You can discover what time of day you're most productive, which websites are distracting you, and how many hours you're truly productive in a day. When a graph is staring you in the face with startling high hours dedicated to social media, you might reconsider your work style and refocus your day. Unless you work in social media of course.

Asana: This online work tool allows for team members to communicate in one space for multiple projects and programs. Instead of keeping track of countless email threads, documents, and calendars. You can track everything and everyone in one location and everyone works in the same platform.

AnyDo: Is a decent task management tool you can keep on your smartphone to keep you focused. It can alert you and remind you to stay on track, especially given that most of us are pretty attached to those devices. Start your day with a list of tasks you've already created, the app sends a nice little Good Morning message to make those tasks seem more pleasant.

Hour Trackers: There are numerous apps that help you manually track your hours for various clients. Freelance/contract workers or those who do more face-time or phone-time with clients than email and computer work rely heavily on these. Hours Keeper is one commonly used tracker available on both iTunes and Android platforms. RescueTime tracks your computer usage. So if you're a website developer it will track your time spent building a website.

IN THE END
You have to like what you're doing. My father-in-law runs a waterfall business in Costa Rica. He leads tourist to some of the most beautiful waterfalls in the country and shows tourists how to cliff-dive into their pools. Almost every tour he's asked, "How did you get a job doing that?" when maybe they should have been asking "How do I create a job doing that?" The next course, *Start a Business From Anywhere* addresses this question.

Additional Resources:

Books: Remote: Office Not Required,
Articles: Why Remote Teams Are the Future,

START A BUSINESS FROM ANYWHERE

When contemplating freedom, it's hard to top being your own boss. The social and technological inventions of the past decade have brought us near the *"End of Jobs"* while making entrepreneurship safer, more accessible, and more profitable than ever before. With a shrinking middle class and no guarantees from our employers why not take matter into your own hands? *"In 2020 there will be 40% more 25– 34 year olds with higher education degrees from Argentina, Brazil, China, India, Indonesia, Russia, Saudi Arabia, and South Africa than in all OECD countries (a group of 34 countries primarily in Western Europe and North America)."* ~ Taylor Pearson, The End of Jobs: Money, Meaning and Freedom Without the 9-to-5

Since 2000, the population has grown 2.4 × faster than jobs. You can see why the last few graduating classes have had such a hard time finding jobs. Maybe it's time you create your job. If you know entrepreneurship is not your cup of tea, then proceed to the next module.

Why think about taking on such a big project and such grave responsibility?

The perks:

- Work from home, whether that's in Bali, Tuscany, or Chicago
- No commute! Unless you want one, in which case, make yourself happy

- Take vacations, sick days, personal days…whatever you need whenever you need it. You are in charge of your own time and your days are yours
- Help out with the family and nurture your marriage (if applicable)
- Enjoy a hike, swim, surf, kayak, or walk during your lunch break (mid-week while the masses are stuck at work)
- Move to a better climate
- Do what you're passionate about and what you hold important
- Change and adapt as your passions and interests change. You can be flexible and continue to evolve your work as it suits you, without having to change jobs or get approval from bosses.
- Rid busy work forever
- Make money doing things you'd usually pay to do. (i.e. If you love playing pool and you start a business as an online pool and billiards retailer it's now part of your job to hang out with your heroes (the top pool players in the world) or flying around the world to speak on your consulting topics such as entrepreneurship or strategy.)

The Cons:

- No steady paycheck
- You are solely responsible for your successes and failures (there is no one else to blame or hide behind)
- Potentially more demanding and most certainly will place you out of your comfort zone

Now is the best time in history to enter entrepreneurship. Not only because traditional jobs are looking grim due to three major shift have occurred that is driving the workforce away from traditional jobs:

1. Drastic improvements in the communication technology sector means companies can hire talent from anywhere in the world (you're now competing with over 7 billion people)! Remember when international calls translated to pay-phones and the purchase of calling cards? Plus, now a new wave of outsourcing is possible.
2. Machines and software have already conquered much of the blue collar job sector and with today's advanced

communication technology much of the white collar workspace is being outsourced. IT, design, accounting, and other jobs are part of the second major wave of outsourcing that began in 2001 and has been accelerating ever since.

3. Traditional advanced degrees are much more common, more expensive, and less valuable than ever before. More and more students are graduating with record breaking debt (B.A. degrees averaging over $35,000 but often up to $100,000 depending on degree and time spent) and jobless.

The Entrepreneur's Work Week

"I had thought that by focusing on business and money I was making myself free, but I didn't understand that freedom requires more balance than that. At that point I knew that if I was going to truly be free, if I was really going to be liberated from work, I needed to focus on ways to reduce the amount of time I spent maintaining my business, and to increase the amount of time I had to focus on what I should really be doing with my life. I knew then that freedom is not just going towards."
~ Erlend Bakke, <u>Never Work Again: Work Less, Earn More and Live Your Freedom</u>

      I learned at an Entrepreneur conference (put on by the namesake's magazine) that at the end of each day you should decide what three tasks you want to complete the next day. That way you can launch into the day focused, diving right into the good stuff.

But what about time zone differences?

      Who says you're glued to a 9am-5pm workday? Maybe a new time zone is exactly what you need to take advantage of mornings to explore a new city or to enjoy afternoons off to catch a wave. Perhaps your ideal schedule will be 5am-1pm. Sure, that's an early start! But if you finish working at 1pm, think of all that daylight time you have for adventures!

      Or maybe you will work 2pm-10pm, which would allow you to sleep in and enjoy a leisurely breakfast before heading out to see what the world has to offer. Key take home message, *"A 9-5 work schedule is not the only option!"* Plus, most industries don't require a response within the same 12 hours, so if you're a few hours off it's not usually critical to your business.

Do I have what it takes to start my own business?

"Everything around you that you call life was made up by people that were no smarter than you and you can change it, you can influence it, you can build your own things that other people can use. Once you learn that, you'll never be the same again." ~ Steve Jobs

MYTH BUSTING

MYTH: "I don't have a gift or talent worth sharing."
BUSTED: Absolutely everyone has a skill, talent, gift, calling…or whatever else you want to call it. You have something others need. You've heard the old adage opposites attract? Listen to what people compliment you on, it's often something they notice because they lack it and they admire yours. We discussed this in the **Retrain Your Brain** module. Many of the worksheet tasks apply not only to your daily life and habits, but to your ability to start your own business as well. Change your daily life and your habits, and you will fly the door wide-open to entrepreneurship.

MYTH: "I'm not qualified to be an expert."
BUSTED: You are more qualified than someone else. You only have to be one step better or further along on a path then someone else to be marketed as an expert. People don't want to be taught by the best in a field they want someone who has put in the sweat equity, someone they can relate with, and someone that will speak to them in a clear concise manner. Someone who will give them the shortcuts they wish they would have had when they were at point A. If you were recently there you can relate in a way the most experienced experts cannot.

MYTH: "Only rich people can afford to start a business."
BUSTED: Starting a business doesn't take cash, it takes guts and the willingness to leave you comfort zone. If your business idea requires initial capital to get started, there are plenty of ways to access those funds. You could start a <u>Kickstarter campaign</u>, reach out to family and friends, or take advantage of cheap cost of living

by relocating abroad to give your budget the breathing room it needs in order to launch your business. Also, plan ahead. Utilize free money saving tools like those offered at www.INGDirect.com where you can set up an automatic weekly or monthly transfer of money into your business nest egg account.

When I wanted to visit New Zealand in my 20s I got a side job where I worked about 10-12 hours a week. I put all of my earnings from this second job into a New Zealand fund. You could do the same for a business account (covering expenses such as business research, training, marketing, and development).

Ideas, determination, expertise, and action are much more critical to the success of a business. There are countless examples of companies started in garages for less than a hundred bucks, Apple Computers being one of them.

GETTING STARTED

Focus on What You Have Not What You Don't Have

Know Your Fundamentals
The most important principle to remember is to focus on what you have. Many people believe you need an MBA or a nest egg to start a business. That isn't the case. You only need three things:
1. A product or service. *"It's easier and cheaper than ever to make something and tell people about it."* ~ Pearson, The End of Jobs
2. A group of people who will pay for it
3. A way to take their money

W.S. 5.1

If Money Didn't Matter
Make a list of what you love doing. List as many things as possible. You know, what would you do if money was not a factor? For example: Dancing, sewing, pouring coffees, giving advice, listening, solving problems, painting, writing, speaking, solving IT problems, throwing parties, fundraising, etc.

_____
_____
_____
_____
_____
_____
_____
_____
_____
_____
_____

Listen to Others

What do people tell you you're naturally good at? Instead of being modest and dismissing compliments from your network, tune in. Pay special attention to what they're saying. When your friends or colleagues say `You're really good at: A) at organizing parties, B) playing matchmaker, C) cooking, D) simplifying the complex, E) running fundraisers, F) interior design, G) making people laugh – listen to what they have to say. They've recognized something in you that you take for granted but they find useful and valuable enough to tell you about it.

Your Sweet Spot

Now take a look at the above two lists and see which areas
people have a need for and already pay good money to have
access to. For example, if you love to cook and have been told by
many that your food is amazing and tastes fresh, or top notch you
might consider a catering business. You can find a model that
satiates your work:play ratio (discussed in detail in the **Design
Your Life** course), such as home delivery 2 days a week, or
special events (but only allow 1 event per week, and price
accordingly).

SWEET SPOT

STUFF YOU LOVE TO DO

STUFF YOU'RE GOOD AT

STUFF SOMEONE WILL PAY YOU TO DO

_____

_____

_____

_____

_____

_____

If at first you don't succeed, don't worry. It usually takes a few failed attempts before you zero in on your best business.

Learn from your mistakes, because it's the secret ingredient to success.

WHAT REVENUE STREAMS DO YOU WANT?

- ☐ **Services**— Like coaching, consulting, copywriting, web design
- ☐ **Products**— Either digital products and programs, books, software, apps, merchandise, instructional videos, and consumer goods
- ☐ **Affiliates**— Promoting others people/company's products, programs or services
- ☐ **Sponsorship**— For events, products, your blog/ podcast/ YouTube videos
- ☐ **Speaking Engagements**
- ☐ **Events**— Workshops, retreats, conferences
- ☐ **Subscriptions**— member only newsletters, blog, Facebook community, access to other resources
- ☐ Other

When considering what revenue streams you want to utilize in your new business keep the work:play ratio you came up with in the *Design Your Life* module. There are passive and active revenue streams listed here. Passive streams pay you multiple times for work you've already completed (i.e. Book sales, product sales). While there is still marketing work to keep sales up, your passive revenue streams are much less labor intensive than active revenue streams, such as: events and services where one sale equal one payment.

Discovering Your Business

If 1,000 fans were paying you $100 a piece annually, what would I do for them?

_____

_____

_____

_____

_____

_____

_____

_____

_____

_____

_____

_____

_____

_____

_____

_____

Do you want the foundation of your business to be based on Passion, People, Problem, or a Product?

_____

_____

_____

_____

_____

_____

_____

_____

Passion: consider which hobbies, passions, issues, industry, or a cause you feel is important to promote

People: think about what type of person you enjoy spending time with.

Problem: observe problems, inconveniences, or needs in your own daily life

Product: Do you know about a product that deserves a wider audience? Or do you have a new product, service, or information that you'd like to market?

If you're stumped here I recommend that you reference your worksheets from the *Design Your Life* course. and take a look at your top ten priorities for work and pleasure and see if it doesn't lean you towards one of these categories.

Write down 5+ business ideas and identify which foundation (P) each would use.

We're just brainstorming so don't be critical, just write the ideas that come to you and test each idea against your Design Your Life worksheets and if you would truly enjoy the work it would take to make the idea a winner.

_____
_____
_____
_____
_____
_____
_____
_____
_____
_____
_____
_____
_____

_____
_____
_____
_____
_____
_____

Whose needs are you fulfilling? How do you reach them
(blogs, forums, noozles, podcast, videos, webinars, apps, etc)?

_____
_____
_____
_____
_____
_____
_____
_____
_____
_____
_____
_____
_____
_____
_____
_____

What are their top needs that you could make money serving? Make certain you understand your audience's preferred method to receive information.

_____
_____
_____
_____
_____

_____

_____

_____

_____

_____

_____

_____

_____

_____

_____

_____

_____

Does your target audience spend money on what you plan to offer? What's their purchasing power?

_____

_____

_____

_____

_____

_____

_____

_____

_____

_____

_____

_____

_____

Narrow down your business ideas to the **top 2**. Test each idea with the following exercises. If none seem feasible head back to step one and start over. The time is much better spent starting over now than later after pouring countless hours and resources into a business that won't pan out. It's just like going fishing. Sometimes you catch one that's underweight and you have to give it back in order to catch the big one. The average business owner has 2-3+ failed business attempts before he/she reaches the one that works for them and their customers.

Check out your competition and similar products or services in other markets. Can you improve on what they're doing? Treat this research like a cafeteria plan. Leave with the best practices of each business model you researched, and mold it into your own business model / product(s).

What key practices did you observe that you want to implement in your business model?

_____
_____
_____
_____
_____
_____
_____
_____
_____
_____
_____
_____
_____
_____
_____
_____
_____

What can you do to differentiate yourselves so that people will want to read your blog, watch your videos, buy your products or services, etc?

_____
_____
_____
_____
_____
_____
_____
_____
_____
_____
_____
_____
_____
_____
_____
_____
_____
_____

Which items, services, or concepts provide you with the best opportunity to make money and align with your top priorities for daily living from the *Redesign Your Life* module?

_____
_____
_____
_____
_____
_____
_____
_____
_____
_____
_____
_____

WHAT WILL IT TAKE TO ROLL OUT THE BUSINESS?

Test your top 2 business ideas against the following questions

How much time and money do you estimate it will take before you're profitable?

_____

_____

_____

_____

_____

_____

What recurring operating costs do you anticipate?

_____

_____

_____

_____

_____

How much of the business requires regular updating (i.e. website, content, marketing, etc)

_____

_____

_____

_____

_____

What can be automated by software?

_____

_____

_____

_____

_____

_____

_____

Can you hire someone else to replace you down the road, or does it require your personal attention?

_____

_____

_____

_____

_____

_____

Is there a way to have your audience contribute much of the content?

_____

_____

_____

_____

_____

_____

How can you scale this business? Will it scale automatically or will you need to pour more resources into it?

_____

_____

_____

_____

_____

_____

THE ONE PAGE BUSINESS PLAN
Cut the crap, leave only the good stuff

Over 90% of wannabe-entrepreneurs get stuck in the transition from business idea to execution. They download a 20 page template for a business plan and get lost in the paperwork, to do lists, and planning. How can you learn from your mistakes if you never take action? That's why we have adopted a one-page business plan to help guide you. Look at this business plan everyday to help you keep focus and work backwards from your goals listed in the plan to the daily and monthly activities required to get there.

Business Name (make sure the domain name is available for your business name and purchase it):

_____

_____

Mission (1-2 sentences):

_____

_____

_____

_____

_____

Business Goals (No more than 5 SMEAR goals)

_____

_____

_____

_____

_____

Actions Required to Reach these Goals

_____
_____
_____
_____
_____
_____
_____
_____
_____
_____
_____
_____

Business Expenses:

_____
_____
_____
_____
_____

Total Expenses=

Income Projection for Each Revenue Stream:

_____
_____
_____
_____
_____
_____
_____
_____
_____

Total Annual Income Projection=

Personal Goals (i.e. What skills do you want to build?):

GLOBALIZING YOUR INCOME

"These days on average people will change their career 8 times before they turn 40... Employers are no longer loyal to employees for their lifetime, nor are employees loyal to employers in the same way."
~ Nora Dunn, The Professional Hobo, a finance and self-sustaining travel guru podcast interview

---

Regardless of whether your business sells a product or supplies a service, you can run it seamlessly from anywhere in the world. Plenty of people are taking their businesses overseas: digital marketers, graphic designers, eCommerce entrepreneurs, online publishers, writers, teachers, etc. You may be well connected, have strong roots, and be happy as a clown in your community, however, this section is for those who are searching for someplace better, different, and beautiful. Maybe it's a different climate you seek, a different pace of life, a new and unique culture, or a more affordable cost of living.

Not only can you save thousands in overhead and improve your quality of life by starting a business abroad, you're also free to explore any destination in the world. Let that realization soak in...

I've lived in Costa Rica, Ecuador, Peru, and traveled through countless countries around the world, all from which I was able to manage and run my business. I can't tell you how refreshing it is to know I can pack up my belonging in just a few minutes and relocate to work in a new exotic country as often as I'd like. For many, bliss comes with the combination of a home-base and a healthy dose of exploration abroad.

There is NO reason why you can't have this too. But before you book your tickets, there is some prep work to be done.

COMMUNICATIONS

You'll need to set up a virtual office system that works. Whether you are working from cafes with wifi or the family home, decide what time of day you're most productive and work your schedule around that time.

Your virtual office could involve being in an internet cafe in any country around the world, on a train, plane, or in a home office in your new tropical abode. Whatever environment you choose, you'll need a reliable internet connection (via wifi or hotspot), smartphone, laptop, and a few applications that will help your workflow. My favorite "office" is a local coffee shop.

Download Skype on your laptop and smartphone. Purchase your own number so you can be reached with a local number while you travel around the world. Depending on your phone habits you can pay for minutes as you use them, or purchase unlimited plans ($2.99 unlimited calling to the US and Canada, or $12.99 unlimited worldwide). I pay $60 a year for my dedicated US number and $2.99 a month for unlimited calling to the US and Canada.

Living or traveling to a Caribbean island, Ecuador, or Thailand doesn't mean you're faced with insurmountable hurdles communicating with your team or clients. In fact, with a Skype number and an unlimited international calling subscription, it's just as if you were in your home country.

Google Hangouts, GoToMeeting, and Skype are all excellent platforms for video conferencing.

Slack is a new program that coordinates communication amongst teams. It's like AOL's Instant Messenger on steroids. With hashtags (#) you can organize and search conversations. So if you need to talk to your graphic designer about a project you can either #project name or #design to organize your conversation. It coordinates with Asana (mentioned below) and a variety of other tools. The best part is it's free!

DOCUMENTS / LOGISTICS

Never has it been so easy to share files with colleagues and clients or even across your own devices.

Dropbox: keep your work documents backed-up and accessible to your team. By saving them on dropbox.com you can share folders, docs, and access them from any computer or smart device around the world. No more headaches when your computer crashes, and you can sell your location dependent file-folders.

Google: Gmail, Google Calendar, Google Keep, Google Drive, Google Docs, Gmail Offline, Google Hangouts and numerous other google apps that integrate with google and gmail will simplify your life, and sync across all of your devices.

Asana: As previously mentioned, is an excellent online tool used to organize projects, to-dos, and keep clear conversations with your staff without the use of email. I used this platform to organize the creation of Life Another Way as well as manage it's daily needs.

It's not likely you'll have access to a Kinkos, and most of us no longer use fax machines, so you may run into potential challenges when it comes to signing documents. Luckily, there are numerous programs that allow you to fax your documents (such as hello fax) from your computer or smart phone, apply a digital signature to documents (Preview on a Mac, Hello Sign on any device). These programs make signing contracts, leases, and other documents a breeze from anywhere in the world. Here is an article that walks you through electronic signatures for those who have never entered this world.

BOOKKEEPING

Being creative and productive is one thing, but it's vitally important to keep track of your invoicing and accounts. You want to see the money coming in.

Freshbooks (starting at $9.95) is an easy, non-intimidating way to tackle your accounting with tools that will track your time, create invoices, manage your expenses and more. Plus, your books are always backed up on their cloud.

Shoeboxed ($10-100 p/mo) is a painless scanning system. Pile your receipts and docs into one of their blue envelopes and send away! Also you can integrate your gmail, outlook, and other email providers so that your receipts are automatically sent to Shoebox, filed, and stored away. They will sort, scan, and organize all of your documents and business cards into an electronic system that will save you time, organize your life, and lift the weight (from piles of paper) off of your shoulders and desk. Moreover, their human data verification makes your documents searchable. They can even create expense reports and track mileage for you through an app on your smartphone.

SUPPORT, OUTSOURCING, & EMPLOYEES

Regardless if you're a solepreneur or you employ an army, creating a virtual team is a no-brainer. Gone are the days when you have to supply a computer, printer, fax machine, and landline to each of your employees. You just saved thousands in overhead with one decision.

You also gave your employees location independence and freedom. Studies show employees who choose their hours are significantly more productive and happy with their job. You can either keep them on as full-time location independent employees or reorganize your staffing needs with virtual assistants (VAs), independent contractors, or outsource your admin and specialized needs. Hiring full-time employees is much more expensive and complicated from an HR standpoint. Take care in your decisions regarding labor and growth of your company.

upwork.com (previously Elance & Odesk), peopleperhour.com, freelancer.com, and fiverr.com (my personal favorite) are excellent websites to find independent contractors or to hire a virtual team. You can pay them per hour or automatically charge your credit card after you've seen and approved their work. That way you spend time doing what you do best, and save the stress and headache of the things you aren't proficient in by hiring those that are. I've personally contracted workers from Upwork and Fiverr that were based out of India and Pakistan. It's been cost effective and incredibly simple.

By creating standard operating procedures (SOPs) for those things you'd like to outsource you can equip others with the instructions to do the work exactly as you'd like them to from anywhere in the world. Outsourcing has been a game changer for the world, and certainly for me.

MARKET RESEARCH

Thank you social media, RSS feeds, Podcasts, YouTube, and every other marketing tool created in the last decade. Because of them you can reach your target market from anywhere in the world for free. Make sure your company creates a detailed social media marketing plan. Learn from your Facebook insights which posts attract the most views and interaction. Pay to boost your most productive posts, starting at just $5.

OVERHEAD

Less is more. Your goal is to rid all leases, landlines, and file-folders. Get used to the idea that your "office" can consist of you lounging in a hammock with a cellphone, laptop, and wifi connection. I've even worked from a beach chair in the sand—risky, and the screen was hard to read with the bright sun, but so worth it! Working from my hammock (covered with a tiki roof) overlooking the pool and the perfectly manicured jungle surrounding it worked out much better than the beach.

ORGANIZING STRUCTURE

There are thousands of various situations and countless ways to manage them. Consult with an international business attorney to see where you should register your business and how you should organize. If you're an international citizen, you might benefit from registering with a country other than your homeland. Recently giant fast food company, Jack in the Box, bought Tony Hortons so they could justify the move of their headquarters to Canada for better tax rates and regulations. Being country-less provides you the luxury to choose where you want to file. Make sure your CPA advises you what tax implications you will face for each potential move both in the country you file in and your country of citizenship.

Taxes for the location independent can get really confusing and the stakes are high. I recently conducted a podcast interview with the owner of <u>Greenback Tax Services</u> and highly recommend you listen to it. Learn about FBAR, Foreign Earned Income Exclusion, and more in laymen terms!

COMMON TRAVEL-SIZED CAREERS

I'll share with you some of the more common travel-sized careers, however I don't want you to think you must enter one of these fields. You truly can travel-size most careers. Even physicians and surgeons are working from home with the help of robots!

WRITING

Freelance writing has long been a career that is ideal for the wanderer. Not only do you have the freedom to design your perfect day on the road but with all of your experiences you'll never run out of things to write about.
Make sure and initiate your writing business from your country of origin. You'll need to build a portfolio and get published numerous times so that you can hone your skills and have a platform to leverage in order to support you while on the road. Subscribe and / or buy The Writers Market. It's a directory published annually that includes the contact information, payment information, topics they publish, and query directions for each publisher. It's basically the writer's bible. If you're hoping to sell some of your images as well then also pick up the Photographers Market, it guides you in the same way to sell your images.

INDEPENDENT CONSULTANT

If you have worked during your lifetime then you have experience in something. Think about what you're good at and see if you can pull together a market you can help through consultations.

There are a variety of business opportunities abroad with new business owners in every sector. These new owners need help with a variety of niches: marketing, social media, customer service practices, IT, website development, content creators, multi-media, international accounting, productivity, import/export, etc.

TEACHING ENGLISH

You can easily earn your TESOL or TEFL certificate online or in the classroom in exotic locations around the world. This certificate makes you eligible to apply for teaching jobs across the globe. Most employers require you to be a native English speaker and have taken a 120 hour course in either TESOL or TEFL. Some also require a Bachelor's degree in any subject.

While taking your TEFL certification, it's possible to specialize in "young learner" or "business English" thereby adding marketability and greater appeal to land a job in your preferred target audience.

I received my TESOL certificate through International TEFL and TESOL Training. I chose the 120 unit course and completed it online with my spouse. They allowed us to turn in one homework per unit since we would be completing it together. Each assignment we turned in was reviewed by our tutor, Earl. If any changes needed to be made, Earl sent it back with remarks. I have no complaints and would recommend them. http://bit.ly/TEFLTESOL

NGOs & FOUNDATIONS

The international NGO (non-government organization) community is enormous. Many of these organizations are in need of English speaking staff in administration, fundraising, marketing, and other job classifications. Monthly salaries can range greatly. Telecommuting from these jobs isn't super popular yet, but you could try to consult for them or work as a temp.

TOURISM JOBS

Tourism is a multi-billion dollar industry. As mentioned before, the baby boomers are just beginning to enter into their retirement as the most wealthy group the world has ever seen. What do they all have in common? They all want to travel. Group travel has always sported a healthy market and is seeing large increases in demand. This means you could hop on an established tour group as a tour director after you earn your certificate through the International Guide Academy: www.bepaidtotravel.com.

Or if you'd rather guide than direct, become a specialized guide for a niche group: LGBT, Food, Wine, Coffee, Grandparent, or Children tours to name a few. You can earn guide certification through the National Tour Association: www.ntaonline.com. In addition to an international license, you might need to obtain your certification as a tour guide from the Ministry of Tourism in your country.

If you're a behind the scenes kind of person and have an artistic eye, you can secure work designing those flashy tourism brochures and website content.

WORK VISAS

Securing a work visa usually requires you to demonstrate that you are filling a position a local does not have the capabilities to fill (i.e. English language, healthcare, IT, Biotech, and International Business skills).

You will need a letter from the company hiring you specifying why they are contracting you and what importance you will bring to their company.

A JOB FOR EVERY STOP

Under the table jobs are offered across the globe in retail, restaurant, hospitality, and tourism sectors. This book does not endorse working illegally, it simply acknowledges that it occurs. Many wanderers gamble with work, banking on their chances at securing work at each location they spend longer stays in. They travel, drain their resources then set down for a few months, save up, and hit the road again. This is self-sustaining and works well for many but is not for the faint of heart. Remember, this method requires you to job hunt under a high stress situation. Being broke is scary, being broke in a foreign country without the means to make it home is even more terrifying!

The people I have seen succeed with this method have been incredibly people oriented. The type that befriends a whole town in a matter of a week. That same skill is what earns them job offers at restaurants, hotels, and housesits.

VIRTUAL OFFICE 101

"When I'm sitting in front of my computer it doesn't really look like work, but it is because it pays the bills."
~Nora Dunn, The Professional Hobo

In order to work from the road, you'll need to establish a framework. This can include but is not limited to setting up an email account, online banking, international communication solutions, business numbers in each country code necessary, mail forwarding services, securing a US address, purchasing a laptop and any other devices required for connectivity to the internet. After the basics are set up, you'll need to figure out when you're the most productive. On planes, trains, in coffee shops, or at home in a quiet space? You will have to be creative with time management so that your work play balance is healthy. Consider what you want your work hours to be. Are you more creative and productive in the morning or late at night? Do you want to treat your travel days like weekend days, or are you productive on the road? You'll need to utilize offline time as best you can. While this world is incredibly accessible to the internet, there are times when you won't be connected while on the road. Applications like Google-Offline are helpful for managing your emails while not connected to the internet. Keep a list of the top 5 things you need to accomplish that don't require internet access.

If in your recent past life you were an 8 to 5'er, it will take some time to adjust to the variety and freedoms allotted to those who work from the road. While it's a great change, it's change none the less. Even good stress wears at you. Be kind with yourself as you find your new groove. Keep making tweaks until you find what works best for you.

Most people feel their best with a regular sleep and rise schedule, a morning shower, eating breakfast, and getting dressed for the day before they attempt to contribute to society. This is still true if you work from home. Just because you can work in your PJs doesn't necessarily mean you should.

Don't neglect your self-care each day. Take time to exercise, eat, and take breaks. It's absolutely imperative that you have a start and stop time! Telecommuting doesn't mandate that you work 24 hours a day. Just because your office and laptop are one room away, doesn't mean you are on call 24/7. You need to set clear boundaries for yourself and those you work with. After all, you're roaming the world to go and explore, you don't want to get caught up working every single day! Creating a balanced schedule and sticking to it is key for a successful balance of life, family, and business.

A friend of mine, Corey Coates, owns a Podcast production company (Podfly) in addition to working for a second company as a program director. He shared,

"I start every workday early with yoga, meditation, and a light breakfast (fruit and yogurt). Then I work until lunch, when I leave for a stroll on the beach. I then return to work until 3:30pm, quitting time. I turn my phone off, close my laptop and don't think of work a minute after 3:30pm. That's the key to being as productive as I am, and not burned out."

ONLINE BANKING

Getting paid is critical!

Paypal— Make sure you can attach Paypal to your bank, and that they allow you to mobile deposit, bill-pay, fax/ wire transfer information, and charges zero or minimal currency transactions fees.

Charles Schwab— offers a High Yield Investor Checking account with no monthly service fees or minimums, no foreign transaction fees, unlimited ATM fee rebates worldwide, mobile deposits from your smartphone, and FDIC insurance up to $250,000!

Flint— is an online transaction tool. You can create purchase buttons to use on your site, you can accept credit cards in person, and can send an invoice link by email.

Square (Cash App)— The Square has been around the block, as the leading credit card processor for small businesses. They recently developed an app that allows you to request and send money via your debit card to a cell phone number or email address. It works flawlessly and is free!

COMMUNICATION

Business would not exist without communication. Your business may require both local and international communication options.

Let's begin with phone communication. Your internet connection is going to be hit and miss on the road. When it's going well Skype and magicJack are excellent options for an international phone solution. Utilizing email and social media to keep up with clients is another nice way around a crummy connection. With Skype you can purchase a phone number with the desired country and area code for an annual fee (my fee this year was $60). You could then forward all of those numbers to funnel through the same phone with the use of Google Voice. If you plan to serve the local community then you need to have an local number, most likely a cell phone for smaller one person operations. This way you can funnel different numbers for different services you may offer.

In addition to a US number, I was given 3 way calling, group video conferencing, and a personal voicemail. As with any internet phone service, there are glitches from time to time. I've had a few instances where my voicemail didn't pick up, and my client was unable to leave a message, but it is a rare occurrence.

With Skype, you can buy a subscription for just about any type of unlimited calling you desire: North America, Latin America, and world wide all starting at $2.99 per month!

If you have a smartphone with a local sim card installed, download the Skype app. Once you are logged in and have a strong connection to the internet through either cellular or wifi, you are able to use all of your Skype features on the go!

VIRTUAL ADMIN SUPPORT

There are a variety of administrative support options available virtually. Packages range from answering services to full-time virtual assistants (VAs). Answering services start at just 80¢ a day including a friendly operator answering the phone with your company's name. Afterwards, they either forward the call or take a message then email and/or fax the message to you. ReceptionHQ has an iPhone app that allows you to change receptionist settings and diversion numbers from anywhere in the world. They offer a free seven day trial. Try them out before you leave the country and see what you think. http://www.receptionhq.com/

A virtual assistant (VA) is exactly what it sounds like, a private secretary that works from his/her home. They can answer and respond to phone calls, filter through and answer your emails, and redirect the ones that require your special attention. Common tasks also include: booking your travel, managing your personal and professional calendar, managing social media, blogging, chat room presence, and running down leads.

Tim Ferriss emphasized the usefulness of VAs in his book The 4-Hour Work Week. One example of a VA company is EAHelp http://bit.ly/USVAs. They provide an executive assistant starting with as little as five hours a week. I have had great luck hiring people from Elance.com, odesk.com, or fiverr.com for administrative and creative tasks.

Additional Resources:

Books: Suitcase Entrepreneur, Start a Freedom Business, The End of Jobs: Money, Meaning, and Freedom Without the 9-to-5, 4-Hr Work Week
Blogs: Jet Citizen, The Perfect Workspace According to Science
Podcasts: Business Basecamp, Suitcase Entrepreneur, Achieve Your Goals

COMPLETE HEALTH

BODY, MIND & SOUL

Before we dive into our method of achieving higher health, turbo charging your energy levels, and raising your mood I want to acknowledge that there are as many correct paths to superior health as their are cultures in the world. The following pages are a compilation of a variety of philosophies and practices that I have tested and found to be effective and easy to stick with, because let's face it, no matter how amazing a program is if it's too drastic or complicated we won't do it.

THE BOD

ALWAYS ACTIVE

Are you an active person or is vegetative a better adjective for you? From now on, you need to make the agreement with yourself that you are an active person committed to your overall health. This means you take the stairs, park far away, or better yet walk or bike to to your nearby errands. Explore the natural assets near you, go on hikes or walks regularly. After dinner walks are one of my favorites. I love walking in the twilight and then ending my walk in utter darkness. It's cool out, there are no crowds, and the darkness is soothing. Bring a flashlight, but most of the time your eyes will adjust and it won't be necessary. Whatever you do find at least one thing to do that's healthy everyday.

If you work from a desk, Starbucks, or your home office it is essential that you get up and move around frequently. There are numerous apps that can help remind you with this goal. You can set them for any time intervals you'd like, but I recommend something between 30 mins to 1 hour. The program I use is designed for Apple computers and is called Dejal Time Out. I select 50 minute intervals and 10 minute breaks. When it's time for a break the screen slowly fads and a picture of the app pops up. You can snooze it once, but try not to do this if you can help it. If there is a song you associate with break time you can set it to play when it's break time. The most important part of this time is that you get up and move. Take time to get water, stretch, or get a quick workout in to help the blood flow back from your butt to your brain. You could run stairs, do some supermans and planks, pushups, pull-ups, sit-ups, or just take the dog for a walk around the block.

Taking these breaks will actually increase your productivity, so if you feel like you're too busy to take a break, realize that the statement makes no sense, and that you're actually too busy to deny yourself a break.

H.I.T.- High Intensity Training

Brought to me by Chris Hammond and based on Mike Mentzer's Heavy Duty <u>High Intensity Training</u> books (HIT) to get strong and fit fast

"You see these guys that spend their whole day in the gym and are here day after day, but how much of their time spent is actually working out, and when does their body have time to rebuild?"
~ Chris Hammond

The question above is what lead Chris to the program I'm going to call *"HIT."* You see, during each workout you're actually tearing muscle strands in order to allow them to build back bigger and stronger. This increased strength and size will increase your body's muscle mass which will makes your metabolism burn more calories per minute no matter what you're doing. More calories burned translates to a slimmer and more defined you.

Chris logically suggests that your body needs at least full four days to fully rebuild the muscle you tore from your last workout, and it needs a ton of protein in order to accomplish this. At the risk of sounding too science-y, the building blocks of muscle are amino acids, which you get from a variety of protein and vegetable sources. In order to build muscle you not only need resistance training, you need a diet that supports growth.

Yes, what I'm suggesting is a 30 minute hard-core workout every five days. Take *that* 4 hour body! I had a hard time believing that this was all I needed to do to gain in strength and fitness. Chris was my Paramedic preceptor at Vista Fire Department and graciously offered to training me to pass a firefighter agility that was particularly challenging. I did everything he said, including eating 1g of protein per pound I weighed (If you are obese, then aim for 1g protein per pound of your ideal weight). You're quickly going to realize this is a ton of protein. In order to be successful you really should eat every 2-3 hours, otherwise you won't make your protein goals and have the constant rebuilding that needs to occur. I didn't have much appetite left over for sweets. See the chart below for foods that are great protein sources and the grams of protein per serving.

This rest and lifting to failure (which we'll talk about soon) system is designed to take each workout to it's fullest potential. You can expect a 10-15% increase in strength each workout!

> *"I noticed my strength/power and endurance ALL increase with HIT, and for the first time I was working out LESS than ever before. That was an ah-ha moment for me! No more of the "dread-mill" and helloooooo 20 minute HIIT workouts!!"*
> ~ Lisa Langenfeld, owner of Lisa Langenfeld Health & Fitness

THE WORKOUT

Mike argued that one set to failure per exercise was sufficient to trigger an adaptive response and that any more exercise would simply be wasted effort and possibly counterproductive in that it would increase the likelihood of overtraining,

> *"...one set to failure is all that is required to stimulate an increase in strength and size – with no number of lesser sets having the same effect."*
> ~ Mike Mentzer (Muscles In Minutes)

Yes, I'm telling you to work out less. Fewer days, and less repetition. Instead, dominate at the gym for just 20-30 minutes of 100% effort, then let your body recoup. Lift with proper technique and a weight selection heavy enough to leave you at failure (i.e. you can barely lift your arms when you're done, or hold onto the steering wheel after your workout) after eight reps of the exercise. For example, if you're doing bicep curls the eighth curl on your right arm should be incredibly difficult and a ninth impossible! The last two reps should be very difficult. At this point the muscle is cooked to perfection and is ready to be left to rest and rebuild with the proper water and nutrition.

It's not all roses, however, while workout out less and for a short period of time is fantastic I would be amiss if I didn't mention how chronically sore you're going to be after H.I.T. workouts. All the more reason to take four full days off of resistance training.

One rebuttal I hear all the time from women is *"I don't want to get all bulky and gross looking."* Not to worry, women's genetics are much different from men's. We don't have the same level of testosterone that muscle men have, there it is highly unlikely that you will bulk in a way you don't enjoy without supplements and/or hormone therapy. Instead, you'll increase muscle mass which will result in a super charged metabolism, lower body fat percentage, and a toned body. Oh yeah, not to mention you'll feel amazing!

While your genetics play a role in how you carry muscle, you can focus on increasing mass in areas that you'd like to see larger, and neglect areas you'd like to slim thereby reshaping your body according to your preferences.

In Muscles in Minutes, Mike advises to life for a duration of four seconds while flexing and another four seconds while extending, with a two second pause in the fully contracted position. There have been a variety of studies that have supported Mentzer's technique.

REST DAYS

Just because your muscles need to recoup doesn't mean you're bedridden. It just means you should stay away from weight-lifting, or other resistance training, and intense workouts. If you want to go for a hike, take your kayak out, go surfing, or walk your dog not to worry you're not breaking the rules. Just don't overdue it. Your muscles need as much of the incoming nutrients as you can give them. If you overexert yourself the nutrients will be redirected and instead of building your muscle you so diligently broke down to it's full potential you'll be shortchanged and potentially fatigued.

FITNESS TO GO

Up until recently, I perpetually made poor health choices while traveling, starting with a McDonalds breakfast at the airport. Once travel became a huge part of my life, I realized I needed to retrain my brain and fix this splurge. I consulted with Yomica Wolfe, an ER nurse, fitness competitor, and fellow travel enthusiast. Here are some of her tips:

1. Be Active

The most important thing is to stay active. Whether travel is your vacation or your lifestyle, the best way to see and experience the country you're in is to be active in it. If you're in a place long enough, sign up for a local race and train for it. Or if you're not a race person, pick out a challenging mountain to climb and work towards conquering it.

"I have run in every single country I've ever visited. From Italy to Greece to Egypt to Israel! Running has shown me so many local shops and neighborhoods I would have otherwise missed! There are plenty of times I've run into an art show or exhibit or something super fun I would've missed out on had I slept in or stayed at the hotel. My personal favorite was when I was in Italy with my ex-husband and I went to a local gym. It was so interesting to see how other people train. The spin class actually took a smoke break!

No matter where you're exploring, look into: renting bikes, swimming, snorkeling, skiing, running, or hiking. Do whatever you can to stay active and dig deeper into the cultural and natural assets a place has to offer. By the end of the day you've had a complete workout and it didn't take you away from enjoying the country!" ~ Yomica Wolfe

Plus as you explore via bike and foot you move at a pace that allows you to absorb your surroundings. Riding in a car is like watching a movie in fast-forward, you're going to miss a lot!

2. Eat Well

"I always stay close to my low fat low carb diet and choose when I'm going to indulge in more. I mostly splurge on alcoholic beverages and let that be my dessert and appetizer." ~ Yomica Wolfe

Whether you're at the airport, on a train, or road tripping in your trusty four-wheeled miracle machine think ahead about what will make you feel good and get the most out of your experiences. Foods high in carbs and refined sugars are going to make you crash and give you a sugar hangover. Most of these venues sell: bananas, apples, grape/ cheese bowl, nuts, and various other healthy options. Also, if you can, pack a lunch with some healthy snacks. Your adventures will be better enjoyed and your friends and family will appreciate your lack of moody behavior that famously accompanies a sugar crash.

3. Water Break

Staying hydrated is huge! Flying in planes, altitude changes, and increased activity can each singularly dehydrate you. Together they can annihilate you. Carry a water bottle with you and drink at least half your weight in ounces daily. While on the plane, drink a glass of water each time they bring the drink cart out. If you have a headache, drink more. The most common cause of headaches is dehydration. If your urine isn't faint in color then you're dehydrated, drink up!

4. Rest /Me-Time

Resting is important too. While being active is key, don't overdue it by setting out to run a marathon everyday, or pushing the envelope with the night life. Schedule blocks of time when you can do nothing, or something that will re- energize you such as: sunbathing, stretching by the ocean, meditating, reading, journaling, and anything else that sounds good to you in the moment. Let this serve as your "me" time. If you're traveling as a couple or group, let this be the time when you break apart to do your own thing so that your needs are the only ones on your mind.

5. Bed Time

Everyone travels differently, but if you spend your entire time avoiding sleep, you'll have one groggy and potentially grumpy experience. Try to get extra rest the first few days to accommodate the jet-lag you may experience. Then, make sure you get sufficient sleep each night. If you have trouble sleeping in a new bed, try playing a guided meditation from your smartphone off of YouTube. Pack ear plugs in case your hotel ends up being too close to a discotheque or you land a travel-mate who snores. Also, if nightlife is a big part of your desired travel experience, pack an eye mask so that you can sleep in a few extra hours to make up for the late night arrival to REM.

6. Get Creative

"I know a lot of people who travel with resistance bands. It's a great idea that I'd like to try myself. I usually do a whole routine with my runs outside, hot or cold: push-ups, high knees, sprints, and hill work (if it's an option). I have one friend that even travels with his road bike!" ~ Yomica Wolfe

Your options to stay active and healthy on the road are limitless with a good sense of creativity. Figure out what you like to do and incorporate it into your travel experience. Even in the dead of an Alaskan winter you could exercise to a P90X video you've saved on your iPhone or go snow-shoeing if the weather allows. If you take care of yourself, your body will take your experiences to a whole new level. Safe traveling!

*Fun Fact: Did you know you can burn up to 40% more calories snow-shoeing than you do running or walking at the same rate?

7. Pace Yourself

A life on the road can be a tiresome one even for a veteran wanderer. Nora Dunn of The Professional Hobo shared how one year she moved locations every 5 days or sooner for a year and how it completely wore her out. Listen to the podcast. Listen to your body, learn your intrinsic pace, and keep making tweaks until it feels right. Hecktic Travels, Pete and Dalene say they like to stay in a country for a few months while they are housesitting, then they travel more quickly and more like tourist for the next month or two then again slow down and get some work done. This pace works by allowing them to recoup and get the bills paid through getting work done for their business. Make sure and give yourself extended breaks in places you enjoy.

"Once you become a little more in touch with who you are and what it is you want to do that natural balance really does predicate your lifestyle a little bit more."

~ Nora Dunn, The Professional Hobo from our podcast interview at www.nomadictales.com

FUEL

"LET FOOD BE THY MEDICINE, AND MEDICINE BE THY FOOD." ~ HIPPOCRATES

Moderation is our friend. While I'm a fan of the philosophies of the Paleo Diet, Diet for Your Genotype, and UltraMetabolism diets, I like to cross pollinate them to find what works best for my body and mind. However, I believe the diet you can stick to which includes fresh foods without preservatives or plastic encasement is the winning diet. Our bodies are ever complex and so unique, which is why I believe that one diet does not fit all. Whichever diet or combination of diets you chose (I will outline their benefits and drawbacks below) give yourself one cheat day a week. It's important to let yourself remain liquid and flow with life. If your diet is overly rigid it will fail. One cheat day a week will also keep your body on it's toes. We don't want to let it get too spoiled now do we? The cheat day can be a different day each week. Just pick a day that works with your social calendar.

DIET FOR YOUR GENOTYPE

As human beings we've seen many shifts in how we live, which is evident in our genomes, or genetic makeup. Scientists have discovered six major genomes which represent different times in our history: hunter, gatherer, and nomad phases to name a few. This philosophy is explained and broken down brilliantly by Dr. Peter J. D'Adamo in Diet for Your Genotype. What I don't like is it's challenging to stick to, and very complex. With the right attitude, it's certainly doable but I find that it is a lot to handle. You're told down to the spice what your body likes and what it has a hard time processing. I do enjoy the insights into what my genotype does well when supported and when I feed it crap, how it acts out. I found it to be very accurate, and the additional awareness has helped me with my overall health. The supplement section is overwhelming. I appreciate knowing what supplements will help which problem, but it was just too much.

THE ULTRAMETABOLISM

The UltraMetabolism teaches you how your metabolism works, and exactly what happens when you introduce high fructose corn syrup or refined carbs into your system. I really wish it was required reading in high school health. Our society would have a much better understanding of how our body works and what fuels it best. In addition to knowledge the book helps you visualize what you're doing to your body when you eat poorly. It's comparable to when you tell a child not to do something, and they ask why, and you explain the negative outcome they are avoiding by ceasing the behavior.

"The foundations of the nutritional principles and the food recommendations in the UltraMetabolism Prescription are two simple ideas that can guide all of your food choices. These are the glycemic load (GL) and the phytonutrient index (PI). Eat foods with log GL and a high PI, and you will ensure a healthy metabolism and optimal health" (Hyman, UltraMetabolism).

Fats and carbohydrates are not created equal. Counting your calories is not an accurate method determine if you're diet is healthy. For example, the fats in olive oil, almonds, coconut, and avocados are not equivalent to the fats found in a pizza or a ding dong bar. There are two main factors you can use when judging if the food you are considering consuming should be part of your diet.

Glycemic Load (GI)

GI is a measurement that estimates how much the food will raise the consumer's blood glucose level after eating it. So, the lower then number the less insulin your body has to produce, and the less risk for blood sugar crashes. The Glycemic Load can also help determine if your body is going to store the food (in your fat cells) or put it to use right away. Foods with higher GIs are usually routed for storage whereas foods with low GIs don't need to be broken down and are ready for use immediately (Glycemic Research Institute findings)

Phytonutrient Index (PI)

In order to understand the index you must know what a phytonutrient is. Basically, it's any compound or substance in plants which is believed to be beneficial and reduce chances of diseases. The PI index measures how many healing properties are in a given food. Almost all refined foods register as zero on the PI index. Phytonutrient foods turn genes off and on relating to your metabolism and chronic diseases. A good rule of thumb is the darker the color of the plant based food the richer the concentration of PIs.

The UltraMetabolism stuff is pretty logical. You'll find that it's philosophies pair perfectly with a high protein and nutrition-rich Paleo diet.

THE PALEO DIET

The Paleo Diet is similar to UltraMetabolism in that it stresses eating fresh foods and produce, but it takes it one step further by asking you to only eat foods that were around during the Paleo time period. This is before the engineered food market began, much before. This means avoiding grains, beans, pasteurized dairy products, and refined sugar. As Diane Sanfilippo states in her book Practical Paleo: A Customized Approach to Health and a Whole-Foods Lifestyle, *"Paleo is Not an RX. Paleo is a template, not a dietary prescription. There is no one cookie-cutter "Paleo diet." If you are eating sole chicken breasts, broccoli, and olive oil, you're missing the point entirely"* (Practical Paleo). She also shares 60-80% of our immune system is located in our gut! When the gut isn't happy with the foods shoved down into it, the inevitable result is sickness and suppressed immune function in a variety of areas. No matter what diet, or combination of diets you choose to incorporate, Diane's statement will ring true for you:

"Know this: we are not smarter than nature. We cannot make better food than nature. We need to at real, whole food—period." Preach it girl!

MIND & SOUL

"You can't run from your problems forever." ~ Charis Enete, a.k.a. my sister

---

Many people won't understand your goal or motivations for your new life. Whether it's life off of the grid, roaming the world searching for the next adventure, or any other variation of Life Another Way. My sister is still trying to wrap her head around my life even though it's been several years. She thinks that because I move around and live in various countries I'm on one endless vacation and am running from "real life." It's ok with me that she doesn't understand, but what is even more important is that I keep up my mental and spiritual health so that her mantra doesn't become a reality.

MEDITATION

There are almost as many ways to meditate as there are religions to practice. As a life guide I will provide a brief introduction to a few methods that will allow you to quiet your mind, refocus your energy, cope with stress, and enjoy the present moment. For all of you who are intimidated by mediation, think it's hokey, or just aren't sure, if you can breath, you can meditate. My favorite mode of meditation is surfing.

ONE-MOMENT MEDITATIONS

I learned about One-Moment Meditations when I stumbled upon a book with that name-sake. I was fresh out of a 5.5 year relationship and was looking to rebuild my confidence and inner strength. Plus, I wanted to be content throughout life's ups and downs, as opposed to a fair weather optimist. I'd never really meditated before, and always pictured it to be grueling. I figured I could do anything for one moment and if it would help my overall health, I'd be crazy not to try. The book taught a variety of meditative techniques that built on one another.

The basic premise is simple, with practice you take a *basic minute* of meditation (discussed below) and slowly cut time until you can achieve the same results in one moment as you can in one minute. With this method you can lower your stress and become present anywhere anytime in just seconds. Look at it as training for the mind much like runners prepare for a marathon. The more they run the quicker they fall into a rhythm and the more efficient their movements are. The more you practice the *basic minute*, the less time it will take to accomplish the full benefits of one moment meditations.

The first paragraph of <u>One Moment Meditations</u> illustrates the need for this practice very well:

"Think of all the moments we 'lose'— stuck in traffic, standing in line, sitting in a boring meeting. Think of all of the moments we 'waste'—going to parties we don't enjoy, working when we're not focused, watching one more television show before bed. Then there are those 'stolen moments'—the moments we grab when no one's looking—to window shop, surf moments that pass by unnoticed—the moments between other moments. What if each of these moments offered us a chance to become more calm, alert, balanced, and content? What if there were something simple we could do in just a moment, that could have a profound effect on our lives?" (Boroson, One Moment Meditation)

The Basic Minute

It's called basic for a reason. No one is too busy to hit the pause button for a minute. Make sure you are free of distractions (close your door, silence your phone, etc). Then set a timer on your phone for one minute, or download One Moment Mediation's <u>free app</u>, which has a timer built in. Sit in a cozy spot with your feet pressed to the ground and your head up, almost as if there was a string pulling the top of your head to the ceiling. Make sure your body feels balanced. Next, simply close your eyes and breath long slow breaths for one minute. When your mind wanders, as it inevitably will do, just simply acknowledge it with a "hmm" and return your focus to your breathing. When your timer goes off, open your eyes and take note how you feel. You'll likely feel a bit refreshed, more relaxed, and more at peace.

The more you basic minute meditation you do, the more relaxed you will feel, and the better you will navigate the space. You can practice this method anytime of day, after you wake up and before bed are great applications. In addition, you can practice it at work wherever that may be. Whether you integrate it into your morning routine (i.e. coffee, set up your computer, basic minute) or during your lunch or midday breaks. You can always retreat to the bathroom to get some peace and quiet if you don't have a private space.

In addition to reducing stress, and refocusing your life to include the present moment, the basic minute will also help you notice when you're not working efficiently so you can take a break and allow your mind some R&R it needs in order to have maximum productivity. Other benefits include:

- Reduction of impulsive acts
- Choosing activities that you are passionate about
- Improved decision making
- Remove limiting perspectives of the past

Think about your newly designed life. When would be the best times to squeeze in a basic minute?

_____
_____
_____
_____
_____

One Moment Meditation

In order to transition from the basic minute to one moment mediation you need to practice the basic minutes at least 5 times a day for a week.

Walking Meditations

This type of meditation is almost like a natural high flooding your senses with the present moment. If you can walk you can take a meditative stroll. Put on comfortable climate appropriate clothes and shoes. The meditation is most rewarding if you can find a place that is out of ear shot of cars, like a large park, the beach, a trail in the mountains or along a river, etc. As you walk focus on your breathing for the first minute or so, then focus on your feet connecting with the earth as you walk. Finally, listen and look for what is happening around you: birds singing, wind delicately whipping through the leaves, trees swaying, the sun warming your face, the sounds of kids playing, frogs, crickets, etc. Focus first on the sounds closest to you and the more you walk focus on every last sound you can detect. Finally, focus on the light all around you. The light illuminated the vibrant green leaves, the light that sparkles on the pound, river, lake, ocean, fountain, or creek

Focused Activity (i.e. surfing, golf, soccer, etc)

Much like walking meditations, you can use an activity to calm and reset your mind on the present moment. I mentioned earlier that my favorite form of meditation was surfing. Let me explain. Waves come in "sets" which can hold 4-6 waves on average, afterwards there's a break called a "lull". Sometime these lulls last ten minutes! Meanwhile I'm basking in the glorious sun sitting on my board which floats atop crystal clear water. The water ebbs and flows beneath me, which causes my hips to roll with the flow of power beneath in order to remain balanced. Looking out toward the endless sea searching for waves provides a deep since of power, and endless opportunity. When the waves do approach, I'm left with utmost respect and attempt to connect with them almost as if the wave and I are dancing a tango. Each change of direction is aimed at returning me to the fastest most powerful part of the wave. The entire ride I must have 100% concentration on the wave and how I can best position myself.

You're not a surfer? No problem. Do you enjoy any sports, chess, cooking, or any other activity that you find your mind lost in? The same rules apply. When I play soccer all sound except my teammates and coach disappear. My concentration zeros in on strategy, anticipation, and execution. If you're mind isn't ALL IN when you're playing a sport or enjoying an activity, then it isn't the right activity to be used as a meditation.

Guided Meditations- Find these at www.LifeAnotherWay.com

- hugging your inner child
- your guardian angel/ best version of you gives you a pep talk
- breath in green healing energy and out black stress, anxiety, and pain

Visualizations

Picture your life another way. What do you look like? Where do you live? What is important in your life? When do you wake up and when do you go to sleep? What does your day look like? Engage your senses, what does it feel like, smell like, what do you hear? Picture these things as if you are already there. What does your work schedule look like? What tasks do you do and what tasks do you delegate or outsource? As you breathe in and out, get in touch with parts inside of you that have the knowledge and ability to make this dream happen. Feel your passion and drive and with each breath feed the fire. Picture each breath taking you a step closer to your dreams. With each breath picture yourself taking a step towards your dream, whether that's going to to gym, writing a business plan, making a budget, etc. Picture the steps it will take if you walk back your dream.

YOGA

Yoga, in it's expression and effect is different from person to person, but it seems to have something to offer everyone. Whether it's the benefits offered by a strengthened core and flexible body (which decreases injury and chronic pain) or your ability to be with your breath in the present moment, yoga is beneficial. Find a balance of what works for you. Do you need to be in a class to feel inspired and to reap the benefits or can you watch a youtube yoga session and get the same results? Some people find great benefit in a daily practice. There is no size fits all so find what works for you between once weekly and daily.

RESTFUL SLEEP

Sleep is critical to our health, energy, and mood. In fact, if we don't sleep well we won't produce the hormones and neurotransmitters required to live a healthy and happy life. You need to prioritize a sleep schedule and discover how many hours is your sweet spot. Mine is seven. If I sleep seven hours, not eight or six I wake up refreshed and full of energy. Sometimes I'm tempted to hit snooze, but every time I succumb to this temptation I awake more groggy that I would have had I just gotten up. Plus, what message am I sending to myself and my intentions for the day? *"I'm not ready for you, I don't want to start this day."* It's like quitting before you start.

SOCIAL OUTLETS

Humans are social beings, some more than others. Happiness is often intertwined with human connection, community, and service. Whether you're nurturing a friendship or relationship, great purpose can be drawn from your addition to their life. You need to discover how often you want to engage in a social activity. Is a weekly game night the perfect amount of social involvement, or is a monthly book club all you have in mind?

Reevaluate, Repeat, Reassess - Life is Fluid

Follow your dreams, they know the way.

Set an alert in your Google (or other) calendar for every week (for the first two months in a new lifestyle), then every month for the next three months, and finally every six months for the rest of time.

Life is fluid, your passions will ebb and flow in and out of your life. You need to be flexible, and check in often with yourself in order to enjoy the ride. This book was designed to be used over and over as your needs and aspirations shift.

www.ingramcontent.com/pod-product-compliance
Lightning Source LLC
LaVergne TN
LVHW020054090426
835513LV00030B/2203